OUR TWELVE SENSES

OUR TWELVE SENSES

How healthy senses refresh the Soul

Albert Soesman

HAWTHORN PRESS

Published by Hawthorn Press, Hawthorn House,
1 Lansdown Lane, Stroud, Gloucestershire, GL5 1BJ, UK
Tel: (01453) 757040 Fax: (01453) 751138
E-mail: info@hawthornpress.com Website: **www.hawthornpress.com**

'Life consists of antitheses'

Rudolf Steiner

The approach followed in this book is based
on compositional phenomenology

Translated from the Dutch, *Twaalf Zintuigen*, UCC copyright notice: © 1990 Uitgeverij Vrij Geestesleven, Zeist, Holland

Acknowledgments
Grateful acknowledgments are made to Ruth Manson, by Jakob Cornelis, for her editorial assistance.

Cover design and typesetting by Hawthorn Press, Stroud, Glos.
Printed in the UK by the Bath Press, Bath.

First English edition, 1990
Reprinted with new Introduction, 1998
Reprinted 2000
Reprinted 2001
Reprinted 2006

British Library Cataloguing in Publication Data
Soesman, Albert
     Our Twelve Senses
     1. Austrian philosophy. Steiner, Rudolf, 1861-1925
     I. Title II. twaalf zintuigen. English
     193

ISBN 1 869890 75 2
978-1-869890-75-9

Contents

Introduction

In spite of startling progress in medicine, biology, chemistry and developmental psychology, there are still mysteries about the human being. *Our Twelve Senses* offers a doorway to some of these mysteries. Here is a guide to entering the very core of our humanity through the most obvious path, the body itself.

In this book the twelve senses are outlined in their activity. But more importantly, Dr Soesman demonstrates how they are involved in aspects of experience not previously ascribed to senses. We are given a look into the nature of the spiritual activities of the senses, and the resulting gifts that each sense brings. In addition, senses are described that are not usually thought of as senses, such as the sense of movement, life, speech, thought or concept sense, and of the sense of the 'I' of the other. Some of these senses are new to us, some seem strange, others obvious.

To look at the human being from unusual angles is not just to perceive things that have never been noticed before. Soesman asks questions about the nature of perception that go beyond physiology. These questions allow us to begin attending to the world in a more particular way, thus giving our perceptions more importance than usual. For example where in the sense of touch does the body end? One might think it ends at the bodily boundary of the skin. But is it not so that if we feel around in the dark with a stick, or cane, we 'feel' to the end of the stick? Or if we are used to driving a small car, and one day borrow the large sedan of a friend, do we not have to adjust our sense of our own boundary to be suddenly much larger than when in our own car?

There is a revival of interest in the senses. Many books are now available on the wondrous qualities of the five senses of smell, hearing, taste, touch and vision. These are remarkable works, some even poetic. But the poetry of the descriptions of the senses sensing, no matter how much the memory awakens to, for example, the first sight of one's newborn, or the lingering ache of the touch of the dearly departed, hardly approaches the senses as bearers of spiritual gifts. Consequently, every book on a particular sense hints at the depth of meaning of that sense, but never makes the final step into the deeper qualities that the sense brings into being. This is where Soesman helps remedy the limited understanding of the senses that prevails. A great secret is revealed here. The senses are the very foundation for the virtues of the soul. We learn at a bodily level, through the senses, capacities for truth, beauty and goodness. We also discover the source of having a conscience, of sensing our destiny, and the capacity to live in community. The senses are more than the simple activity of perceiving; they are indeed the foundation for the soul to express itself through the body.

This book opens the door to many of the mysteries of human development. This new understanding helps us begin to treat one another as whole human beings, not just the symptom of this or that behavior. What does this mean? For example, if a child cannot seem to learn to read, experts might well diagnose dyslexia. We schedule the child for remedial work in reading, and slow the whole process down, or even go back to the beginning. We build on what has been discovered in the past 20 years or so in the science of education.

When a child begins to read it is not just the letters, sounds and meanings that are engaged. It is also the sense of movement. The sense of movement, described by Dr Soesman so eloquently in Chapter Two, must work in a healthy way to make it possible to learn to read. This sense is so innate, so basic, that we do not experience it as a sense so much as a naturally given ability. But this books helps us come to see it as a sense and learn the qualities of that sense. We can now realize that movement as a sense can affected adversely and become disturbed. The disruption can have repercussions far beyond whether or not someone is graceful or clumsy. One could observe the child having difficulty reading as not being able to follow the movement of the letters as form, as combinations, as proceeding across a page. In addition to the letters forming particular shapes, shapes that combine into particular groups, and groups that line up in orderly sequence, there is the eye that must follow, the body that must hold still.

The sense of movement can be – and is – enormously disrupted in our time. For everyone. The causes of disruption include, for example, the oscillating, low level, electro-magnetic fields emitted by TV's, computers and household appliances. No one can escape such disrupting forces, yet some are more affected by them than others.

Could this increase of electromagnetic activity contribute to dyslexia? Electrostress affects very subtle aspects of the sense of movement. So the connection between electromagnetism and dyslexia may not he so far fetched as it might first sound. In addition, our movements are the reflection of the movement of the world around us, and so are delicately related to our environment. As the infant's capacity for self directed movement develops, the child imitates the activities of other people. When we as adults move in relation to the sounds of electrically reproduced voices and music, we move differently than when we move in relation to the subtle rhythms of nature. Movement becomes more mechanical, less rhythmical, and more robotic.

The environment of the young child can offer a calm atmosphere that allows the unfolding of the rhythmical grace of the human body. But the child's movement can also be restrained by the sound of electrically simulated voices moving to the incessant beat of time unrelated to body rhythms. Children are very sensitive to the nuances in their environment. They cannot distinguish between sounds that are related to healthy movement, and those that can be destructive. We see many children affected this way, and rarely recognize the cause. For example, a mother who sings her child to sleep, or tells a story, soothes the tension and excitement out of the child's body, allowing for relaxed, restful sleep. Children who go to sleep with recorded music, the television or even a taped story, fall asleep from exhaustion. The ongoing stimulation does not allow for restful, relaxed sleep. and children become easily irritated, poor eaters and lose patience with their environment quickly.

This is an example of the profound possibility for new understanding offered by coming to the twelve senses. We take our perceptions seriously, if not very consciously. The sense of movement dictates not only whether or not we learn to read easily, but even whether or not we form relationships. For as Dr Soesman suggests, the sense of movement has the surprising task of giving us a sense of our destiny. It gives us a sense of life direction, of orientation. Why are we here? Can this truly be answered by understanding what is sensed in movement? And if this could be known, would we not live here differently, perhaps more consciously, with others? Here we come to the border of a new knowing, a knowing with more of one's being than the prevailing dualism.

The relationship of the senses to the deepest mysteries of goodness and evil, love and hate, progress or mass destruction is obvious when we realize that the senses are the foundation for those qualities that we hold most dear. The sense that we are basically good, we can trust and be trusted, that beauty is inherent in us as well as in nature, are qualities we long for in the hopelessness of increasing violence and greed. No single one of the senses with its particular disruptions can he pointed to as the exclusive source of social ills. No one of the organisations we expect to fix things can heal the senses. The disruption is in them all, in us all. And the healing we yearn for can only happen at the individual level. The world is not in dire need of a new educational system, honest politicians or family values. It will not be made safe with reformed corporate greed, more policemen or soldiers, or a return to fundamentalism. The simple act of nurturing the senses might well do far more for the healing of the world than all our programs and inventions.

We begin to see that the body itself carries the capacity to heal the world, if we understood and lived in balance with the gifts of the senses. The attack on the senses deadens the experience of living in our bodies. The senses can give us the capacity to recognize aspects of the world that are the source of disruption. But we are not awake to these subtle indications. We do not ask the right questions, we do not look in the right places for answers to the human condition. In looking outside ourselves, we miss the only domain that holds the secrets. We can only bring about the changes we seek for social reform from within our individual selves. We can only bring about the changes we seek for social reform from within our individual selves. We cannot progress otherwise. It is not a matter now of knowing more, but rather of developing the capacities of perceiving truly. This is a task for everyone.

It is unlikely the world condition will improve quickly. With continued disruption of the senses it will in all likelihood regress. How much longer can we go on in the dark? The hardest thing to do in our time is to transform our consciousness. But what if we could bring balance into our perception? This book is a guide. From this point on we have no excuses for not re-creating the world to be a harmonious place. We must awaken to our senses not by knowing about the mechanics of their physiology, but in our senses by knowing imaginatively 'through' them, the world and ourselves.

When Rudolf Steiner researched the senses early in the twentieth century, the world still retained a certain balance. But I do not think even Steiner could have predicted the sensory havoc caused by technology and the shifts in the social environment. As we make the world speed up beyond the speed of sound, we greatly alter the sense of hearing. We lose the ability to see what is before us with the enormous increase in visual stimulation and simulations of images into picturings. Similar changes have occurred with all of the senses.

Perhaps our greatest folly is to forget that the world is not simply to be manipulated and consumed. Do we wonder what has happened to the world when we lose the ability to perceive it as part of ourselves, and not just as an object outside of our body? Once the world has been placed 'over there' so to speak, we also place the human body 'over there' as object. The world is more distant, but so is our own body, our very humanity. The senses are not just the foundation of our relationship to the world; they are intimately entwined with the world, making and unmaking reality. If we remain unconscious of the world that is given through our senses we may never be able to find the deeper meaning of why we are here, what is our task, how we can help. At this point in time, the meaning of life can no longer be just what happens next. We must take hold of the fact that our senses themselves are what give us the ability to be human beings, and therefore to create a world. Then, perhaps, we can begin to consciously bring healing and balance back into the realm of the senses, and into the world.

Perhaps no other book will be as important as the one you now hold, if you have any feeling for the earth, for others, for the future. This is because it leads us to develop the senses we are most unfamiliar with, the higher or spiritual senses. These are the senses of hearing, speech, concept and the ego. The development and unfolding of these senses can help realize the opportunities for healing we seek. These senses are just beginning to manifest in us as senses.

The spiritual senses are less familiar, but we can recognize them. One example is when we travel to a foreign country. We experience a new landscape and hear strange sounds. We have no idea what it is we are hearing, except that it is human language. The perception of language, human speech, as sense ability is a part of us and yet is not so recognized as a sense. We are also able to sense the activity of thinking in the other, of the presence of the individuality, the 'I' of the other. It is surprising to think that as we awaken to these senses, we will discover deep spiritual truths, including the nature of true community.

With the direction given by this book, inner knowing can awaken, and lead us to our true humanity. The world will become a more sense-able place, for only through us can harmony and balance be restored. The path is through coming to our twelve senses.

Cheryl L. Sanders, MS
The School of Spiritual Psychology
Great Barrington, Massachusetts, 1998

Preface

During the past several decades I regularly gave courses and talks about the senses based on the work of Rudolf Steiner. On such occasions I was often asked whether I could not write a book on what I had spoken about. Apparently many people are intrigued by Steiner's view of the senses (after all, we are concerned with our senses every single moment!). But many people can hardly, if at all, cope with the material on this subject in the stenographic reports of Steiner's lectures. This is the more regrettable because Steiner did not, as is customary, distinguish five senses, but as many as twelve.

Still, I always said "no" to the request from course participants and from my audiences. This was partly on account of my work as a family physician, which did not allow me to take the time to commit my thoughts to paper, but partially also because I had found that I felt much more at home with the spoken word than with the written word. As a speaker you can respond to the reactions of your audience, to their questioning faces, their yawns, and so forth. As a writer, you don't know just whom you are talking to.

The requests for a book became more urgent as time went on, however, so that finally, after much hesitation, I gave permission to have the text of one of my evening courses, which had been tape-recorded, edited and adapted to a book format, with the stipulation that the character of the spoken word would be preserved. The result of this gigantic effort, undertaken by the publishing firm Vrij Geestesleven in Holland, is this publication.

I sincerely hope that the reader can put him- or herself in the place of the listener on a chair in the auditorium. Much of what I have to say should be taken as imagery. Together with my listeners I always try and gradually build up an image to its final completion. As in clay modeling, it is a formless mass at first, which at some stage begins to take shape, slowly but surely. The final form, the correlation between various components, and the internal proportions become visible only when the whole sculpture is finished.

Specifically, what I have tried to do in this course is to relate and clarify what Rudolf Steiner disclosed about the senses in a difficult series of lectures he gave on October 23, 25 and 26, 1909, in Berlin (Gesamtausgabe No.115: *Anthroposophy—Psychosophy—Pneumatosophy*) and to do it in such a way that the subject matter becomes understandable for anyone. I have attempted to choose my approach and my examples in such a way that those who are not familiar with anthroposophy can find an entry into this world view. (In this respect this course can be considered to be an introduction to the anthroposophical image of man.) At the same time I also hope to interest and inspire those who have already studied much of Steiner's work.

Readers of this book will find that for each sense I give some indication about its relationship to a specific sign of the zodiac. Those who wish to know more about that subject may find more information in the lectures given by Rudolf Steiner in Berlin June 20 and July 18, 1916 (Gesamtausgabe No.169: *Weltwesen und Ichheit*).

Finally, I want to draw attention to the synopsis included at the back of the book. Although one always runs the danger with this that something that has been presented in an imaginative and living way may become rigid, and even though it is very difficult to put the senses into a schematic form in any event, I still felt this should be included. Those who find this of help can then review one thing and another in summary fashion after studying the six lectures.

Albert Soesman

Chapter One

The sense of touch and the life sense

I want to try to give an introductory course in anthroposophy in six installments. There are many ways to approach anthroposophy. The way I propose to do it is to take a particular subject as my starting point. You can start with anthroposophy in general and make your way from there into a specific subject, but, interestingly enough, you can also start with a certain subject and work your way up from this into anthroposophy as a whole, in as far as it is possible to arrive at a general outline of anthroposophy in six lectures. I hope your souls will succeed in following this reverse path — starting with something specific in order to end up with something general.

As was announced, the following will be based on the studies of Rudolf Steiner. Rudolf Steiner once said that a study of the senses is actually the first chapter of anthroposophy. While that sounds simple enough, I will have to start by saying something first about that word 'first'. Usually, when you read an ordinary book, and you have read chapter 1, you are then finished with chapter 1. Next comes chapter 2, and subsequently chapter 3, etc. That is, in fact, how many books are written. But by no means all books are written like that. When you read *The State* by Plato, for instance, you will find something very peculiar about that book. Its structure is not: chapter 1, chapter 2, chapter 3, etc.; instead, reading that book is like walking through an immense temple building, as it were. The whole book is structured like a Greek temple; it is not just a sequence you follow. And this is often also the case with the work of

Rudolf Steiner. You have to get used to this at first — that in fact everything, to the last chapter, is already contained in chapter 1. And it is the same in chapter 2 — everything is already there.

This is also how it will be with my lectures. So you will have to bear with me. For some of you it will seem strange that I do not follow a logical sequence — that you have to learn to consider matters in a compositional fashion. You will have to have some patience, and be prepared to wait and see whenever I say something that seems unusual to you. You will have to let go of linear thinking to some extent. I hope you will find that when something seems strange to you, the next thing may, in fact, balance it out. You will have to look upon these lectures as a piece of music. When you listen to music, you do not think: 'All right, here is the first tone, now where is the second, the third?'. Instead you simply wait until the entire piece is finished, and then you can say: 'That was terrible', or: 'Yes, it did something for me', or whatever. That is the sort of consideration I ask of you — to bear with me until the compositional element makes an appearance. I know I am asking a lot of your patience, but I hope that in the end you will find it worthwhile.

So, what we are going to talk about is the senses. It seems like a nice way to enter into anthroposophy. You are all sufficiently familiar with Rudolf Steiner to know that he liked to speak about the spiritual world and that he leads us onward to tremendous heights. On the other hand, you could not imagine a more practical person than Rudolf Steiner was. He could give advice on the most practical, every-day matters, and, in fact, he opened our eyes to many practical, every-day matters. That is why a study of the senses is a nice way to get into anthroposophy. Everything I say can be verified. After all, what we are talking about are our every-day senses!

Anthroposophy encompasses a spiritual science that attempts to complement natural science from a particular point of view. Therefore, I will bring in a lot of material from natural science and demonstrate to you that many riddles in natural science can be solved by adding a spiritual component. Perhaps I will relate many things you already know all about, but perhaps you have never seen them in this context.

You know we all have a number of senses. Just to name a few: sight, hearing, touch. They are only too familiar to you. What is far less well-known is that these senses are connected with each other. What was so totally new and original about the contribution of Rudolf Steiner was the idea that these senses constitute an order, or, to use an old, and apt, expression of Pythagoras: together they form a *cosmos*. A cosmos is a well-ordered whole. This is the surprising outcome that can emerge after we have worked together six times or so, namely that one thing is inseparably connected with another, and that together they make a tremendous, wonderful composition. And only because of this composition can you gain an understanding. You can not really describe any one of the senses without being familiar with all the others. That, in fact, is what is new about this. That is why I can not arbitrarily deal with one sense here and one sense there. I have to take this cosmos, this general order, into account.

I will start by enumerating this order. Then at least you will know what we shall be talking about on these six occasions. I will begin with something quite familiar — the sense of *touch*. Then there will be something that is probably new to you: the *life sense*. Then comes the *sense of self-movement*. After that a well-known phenomenon again: the *sense of balance*. Next comes *smell*, then *taste* and *vision*. Then we come to the *temperature sense*, and after that *hearing*. Following this there will be a number of senses probably still unfamiliar to you, namely the *speech* — or *language sense*; the *conceptual* — or *idea sense*; and finally the *ego sense*.

If you number these, you come to 12. You can already see that this is a cosmos — these 12. But I will have to explain to you why this is so. Once you become familiar with this concept of 'cosmos', you will understand that man does not have just any number of senses, that it is not as if he might as well have a few more or a few less. Of course, we can imagine all kinds of things. We can easily imagine a man on the moon. Too bad, but there is no man on the moon, and neither on Jupiter. We can imagine anything we like. But if we want to come to grips with the concept 'cosmos', we shall see that there can be only 12 senses, no more and no less. That is simply what a cosmos is like.

Today I want to start with the sense of *touch*. You all know it. We all can touch something. And now we immediately have a problem. I have already said: in order to understand one sense, we have to concentrate totally on that one sense. I have also told you, however, that this is impossible, since each of the senses separately is only understandable by bringing in the other senses. There we have a big problem, indeed. You can see it right away when, for instance, I touch this table. I feel the table, and it is cold. Yes, but that is not touch, that has to do with the temperature sense. At the same time as I touch it, I push myself away from it to some extent. I change my balance. Sure, by the effort of changing my balance I become aware of something. But then I do not only use my sense of touch. I need my sense of balance at the same time. Of course I can also run my hand over the table and then I become aware of whether it is rough or smooth. Even though it is somewhat more difficult to grasp (I shall come back to this later in more detail), all I want to say is that with this last action I have engaged my sense of self-movement. That is the sense with which I notice my own motion. As you can see, a sense never works on its own. It always needs the help of other senses. What makes this concept a little difficult is that in our thinking we have to let go of all those other aspects that come into it when a sense is active. We have to try and concentrate on the secret of what, really, is that one sense — touch.

Try and imagine it working all by itself. What does it show? What does it actually reveal to us? Which gate of the soul opens up? Into what realm do we enter because of that one sense?

With the sense of touch I do not feel whether something is warm or cold, whether it is rough or smooth. I do not notice my balance changing. What is it I actually become aware of, then, when I use touch only, leaving everything else out? What am I

left with, and what does this tell me? Let us do an exercise. We
first have to turn off the lights, for usually when we touch
something we also look at it. Now we should try, in the pitch
dark, to be a being of touch only. I beg your pardon, but would
you please try and be a naked worm? Imagine a worm, only a
worm in the pitch dark. The temperature around this worm is
the same as the worm's own; it does not feel warm or cold. But it
does not simply slide around everything. You can try it yourself
tonight, without your pajamas on. It is rather difficult to do this
in your own room, for as soon as you bump into a chair you see
that chair in your mind. So, tonight you all have to move to a
strange room. Only that way will you, for the first time, get
some idea of the way the sense of touch works, in a totally
unfamiliar environment, without recognition or memories. In
this way you enter a new world, which you crawl into, totally
naked. And this for the first time in your life. Imagine that! It is
not easy, for we are so used to coming into contact with things.

What is the word for this? Any word is already too complicated.
But we can not escape the fact that we are tied to thinking,
which always uses words. What would it feel like when for the
first time you experienced touch. Resistance? Yes, you would
indeed feel resistance, something dragging. But would you feel
anything else? Nothing at all. That means 'resistance' is much
too complicated a word. Resistance already goes too far, actually.
There is, really, only one word — even though it is not quite
right either, for in each word the activity of many senses comes
together — one word you can think of in this connection, which
is it. You see it, don't you, if you had no senses at all, and for the
first time you had this sense of touch, and you 'wormed' up
against this pebble, you would experience something: 'It'. And
what would happen next, if you had no other senses and you
were 'worming' against something without knowing what?
What would you experience? Resistance? You haven't come to
that yet. 'It'? You can see, can't you, there is something of a first
'awakening'. Let me put it this way: This resistance comes from
outside, but something also happens in the human soul when
we come into contact with something, even if only as a worm for

now: *We wake up*. Now, waking up is a very complicated process, but a very tiny bit of becoming conscious — again, each word is much too complicated — something of a first awakening to the world — that is what happens. You get the general idea.

Now you have experienced something quite peculiar. You come into contact with something, somewhere in the world, but at the same time you make contact with part of yourself. This, actually, is the remarkable thing about touch, namely that part of myself, something within me, awakens to part of the world, something in the world. I hope I have made it more or less clear.

You can see that this 'awakening' is related to a certain phenomenon, namely an *awareness of a boundary*. Suddenly we become aware of: boundary against boundary. That is more or less what happens. Slowly but surely we become conscious of our boundaries. You have to imagine that this happens very gradually, in fact. Regrettably we know very little of how all this took place when we were small. You can simply put the theoretical question: Does an infant know where its crib begins and where it begins itself? Does it know where its little hand begins and where it comes into contact with the crib? It is astonishing when you ask yourself this kind of question. For then you realize that an infant does not know this, of course. It has to learn this slowly, bit by bit; it has first to bump into the crib a hundred times. This takes place by means of the sense of touch.

The human being goes a long way in this. Many animals do not go nearly as far. Observe a sea anemone, for instance, with its small mouth, and many tentacles, which it can retract. It is amusing to see a fish come into contact with these tentacles. The sea anemone is startled, and everything contracts, but then it unfurls again, until the tentacles come into contact with a stone. Again the sea anemone is startled, and again pulls in its tentacles. It continues doing this until finally it 'dares' to touch this stone. A worm never reacts like this. If a worm bumps into a stone, so what? But if you touch a worm with your finger you give it a start. In other words, a worm is more advanced. It makes a difference whether something touches it or whether it touches something. You see the difference? If a pebble hits the worm it gives the worm a start, but if the worm touches the pebble, it remains undisturbed, and crawls onward. A sea anemone never learns to do this. The sea anemone is given a start again and again when it touches something. It has to take its time, each time, to experience: 'Do I touch something, or is something touching me?' So you see that a polyp does not yet have quite the same degree of boundary awareness with respect to its own body as the worm does. One is not all that low on the scale being a naked worm!

A remarkable learning process, which you have to imagine dramatically, is that of discovering: 'How did I come into the world, and how do I get to know how large I am? Where are my boundaries?' Something on the outside keeps knocking against some part of my body surface; this is how I find out about my circumference. This is a laborious process that takes years and years, starting with birth. I am convinced that this has a deep connection with the sense of touch.

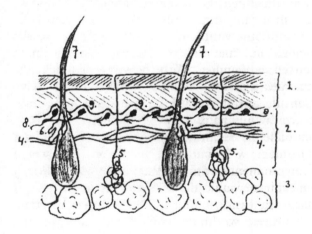

1.	Epidermis	6.	Sebaceous glands
2.	Endodermis	7.	Hair
3.	Subcutaneous tissue	8.	Nerves
4.	Vascular system	9.	Tactile corpuscles
5.	Sweat glands		

Sectional view of the skin

Now, when you have the large-scale picture, you will also begin to understand the small-scale picture. The sense of touch, you see, is constructed quite simply. In the highly simplified drawing you see the epidermis, the dermis and the subcutaneous tissue with all of the bloodvessels, sweat glands, hair, etc. There are nerve endings, which end in the so-called tactile corpuscles. Our sense of touch is not constructed in such a way, therefore, that it 'sticks out of the skin'. There are no protruding nerve ends. If the sense of touch was constructed that way, we would never experience a boundary. We shall come back to this later on, and then you will see the connection when we talk about smell. Smell, you see, *is* built that way; with smell you never have the sense of boundary-to-boundary. That is specific only to the sense of touch. With touch you do not end up in another world, the outer world; you stay in your own world. You really have to think of it as a boundary situation. And the surprising thing about the sense of touch is, really, that it does not tell us anything about the other world. We only experience 'it'; we experience only that there has to be another world, and that we somehow wake up to this other world. With touch you never really enter the world; this world, put simply, is used only to make you self-conscious, and that in a bodily way. You begin to experience yourself as bounded. With the sense of touch, the small infant separates itself from total unity with the cosmos. It is a withdrawal from the cosmos in order for the infant to begin to experience its own bodily nature, slowly but surely.

This way you suddenly see the meaning of a sense. If we did not have the use of touch, we would all be totally one. We would dissolve in the environment as a drop of water in the ocean. Even if we had elephant skin we would still feel like a drop in the ocean if we did not have the sense of touch. For in order to attain consciousness you need two things, which I will show you in a drawing.

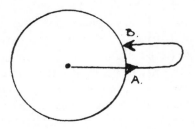

Imagine you are at one with the cosmos. You would then be totally asleep, you would have no consciousness in this cosmos. Imagine that for some mysterious reason you departed from this cosmos, and that you became totally separated from it. You would still have no consciousness. You would be a lost soul without consciousness. You only gain consciousness if you leave this cosmos and then immediately bump into it again, as is indicated primitively in the drawing: You first go this way (arrow A), and then you return (arrow B). If this cosmos simultaneously closes itself off from you, then, and only then, do you gain an experience of yourself.

I am telling you an old story: that once we were one with the cosmos, and that subsequently we left it. From a certain point of view, all human striving is nothing else but knocking on the door of the house from which we have been evicted. There is nothing tragic about this, for because we have been thrown out we do, in fact, gain consciousness of ourselves. What is quite peculiar is that when we gain self-consciousness, we are outside something.

The sense of touch has a quite definite task for the human being. We are released from the divine totality, and simultaneously the desire arises to return to it. We have continually a deep longing to touch things. Even in the language it comes to expression when we say, for instance: 'The tension is tangible'. We mean the tension was so strong that we could touch it. You can imagine, I think, the situation when you meet someone who you believed had died; you really only believe that he is for real

when you have touched him. By means of touch we gain
certainty about something. We get a sense of a thing in our own
'thing space' — that is what the sense of touch is. That is what is
hard and fast about touch — things are separate.

But at the same time we use touch in quite a different way as
well. We use it not only in order to experience whether something is really there or not, but also to express *intimacy*. When,
for instance, a pretty child comes along, with the sun shining on
its hair, it is almost impossible not to stroke that hair; one really
wants to stroke it. Then suddenly one uses touch in a very
intimate way. It is funny: we use the sense of touch by turn in
quite an objective way and to express intimacy. We have to be
careful not to confuse the two. When, for instance, a doctor
examines a patient, when he examines, say, the abdomen of a
patient — when he is looking for a tumour, for example — he
does this quite objectively until eventually he feels whether or
not there is something amiss. The physician has to be careful,
however, that he does not touch the patient in such a way that
something else entirely enters into it. It is then up to the patient
whether he wants to stay with that doctor or not! The doctor can
in such an instance be diverted to a totally different aspect of
touching.

There is a peculiar paradox in the sense of touch: on the one
hand you can feel that a piece of wood, for example, is something
hard, but on the other hand you can feel that it is a fine piece of
wood. You can feel: How beautiful it is, doesn't it feel good
when you run your hand over it. This is the peculiar thing: In
the hardness we experience being excluded from it, and in the
pleasure of touching we experience the desire to make an
intimate connection. In this we see an innate desire of the
human being; he actually knows that the sense of touch separates
him, excludes him from something, to which he is yet
related. We are not totally closed off from the cosmos, this is
what I mean. If we were, in fact, totally outside the cosmos, we
would have no longing for it whatsoever. But because we
continuously bump into it, because we hug it, there remains in
us this desire to reconnect ourselves with that real world, with

which we were once bound up. The sense of touch, therefore, really establishes a boundary, a separation. We became loosened from the totality, and we ended up snuggling up against it, as it were.

Why, Novalis says it much more beautifully than I can explain it, when he states: 'Touching is separation and connection both at once'. This is one of the deepest secrets of the cosmos. It is the thread that runs through our entire evolution − this release from the totality, this separation; but at the same time this feeling that remains in the human being of being connected with it after all. It is no coincidence, therefore, that the sense of touch is most acute in the fingers. It is really remarkable that with our fingers we can touch ourselves all over. You will say, 'Yes, but I can do that with my eyes, too'. But with your eyes you can only touch part of yourself. With your sense of touch you can touch yourself everywhere. That is the special secret of touch. You can use it to outline yourself as a self-contained unit. In actual fact, just as you can walk around the earth, so you can walk around yourself with your sense of touch. A baby can not do this. An infant has to be 2+ or 3 years of age before it can accomplish this. It is only when the child really starts saying 'I' that its arms have become long enough and its proportions such that it can touch itself all over.

There you see the great secret of the sense of touch, the sense of boundary, which brings 'us' to a first awakening to 'things'. Obviously, this sense plays an enormously important role in the upbringing of children. For coming out of paradise into the world can take place in many ways. I will give a simple example: There has to be an enormous difference for a child between touching the mother's breast, and a bottle. It must be obvious to anyone that there is a difference. You have probably heard about children who have no immune resistance, who have to be brought up in a glass cubicle; they never have the direct contact of touch, of caress. It remains to be seen how these children will react at a later age, having been so drastically excluded from the world of contact because of a tragic physical condition.

How marvelous it is, on the other hand, when as a child you

are always cherished by your mother, your father, or other people – that you are caressed by them, and that in this way you are being helped by them to leave paradise without losing this basic desire to return. As of old, people have known that it is good to play tickling games with children. 'Round and round the garden, goes the Teddy Bear; one step, two steps, tickle him under there!' What an incredibly deep significance has such a game! For that is how you gradually teach the child about the separation from paradise. It is funny, but a very small child is not ticklish. You have to be older for that. You have to have become detached from paradise to some extent before the mother's hand can really tickle. And yet it is a wonderful sensation, this tickling, which only later becomes real tickling. You can never tickle yourself. That would be great, wouldn't it? Imagine, when you feel sad all you'd have to do is tickle yourself. But that does not work at all.

All of these simple daily things have a profound background, and that is what is so marvelous about anthroposophy. What matters in anthroposophy is really not the ascent to loftily high worlds. These high worlds surround us on all sides. You can think for a long time about why it is that you can not tickle yourself. It is a very profound matter that only something foreign can tickle you. You are not foreign enough to yourself, as another human being is. That is the whole thing. And all of this has to do with our sense of touch. Just think what a difference it makes whether a child comes into contact with fine things, such as good wooden toys and soft woollen or silk dolls, or whether it plays mainly with plastic toys. There is a vast difference in the quality of the touch sense developed in a child that is brought up with natural materials from that of a child that has grown up with quite another kind of material. There is no greater imaginable difference than that between a machine-made jumper and one knitted by grandmother.

And thus we return again to the paradox of touch. It forcibly expels us from the world, even if it takes years; we then confront the world, and at the same time there still is this strong, intimate urge in us to reconnect ourselves with the world. But in touch we always experience the disappointment of never really getting inside this world. Because of touch, in fact, the world becomes a riddle. You experience this when you have something in front of you, such as, for instance, a beautiful stone. You can feel it, and when you touch this stone it opens up for you, as it were, a wonderment about the world. You touch it and you realize: 'I have it in my hands, and the riddle becomes greater and greater now that I have in my hands a piece of the world; I have an amethyst in my hands, and I feel that it is an amethyst. I am so close, but the closer I get to it, the further I am away from it. An approach to the spirit is really possible only by way of an inner path, such as that indicated by Rudolf Steiner in, for instance, his book *Knowledge of the Higher Worlds and Its Attainment*.

Rudolf Steiner said the following about the ultimate secret of the sense of touch: that the human being would never become conscious of the divine without the sense of touch. We could never be religious without touching. For as soon as we touch something we have the magic feeling: this is a world to which I said good-bye, and which is beyond understanding. This is what we call the metaphysical. Hardness against hardness. We are so close, and at the same time so far away. It is from a bodily basis — for it is all developed out of our bodily nature — that we come to an awareness of the divine. We could never do this otherwise. And we will see time and again that all of our senses are great teachers of man if only he will open his spiritual ear to this. We can philosophize as long as we want about God, whether this is a fantasy, for example, because you have a father, of which God is a Freudian projection. But if you ponder on the sense of touch, you come to the most definite inner experience that with the development of touch man can, at a later age, when he can think, come to the realization that a divine world does exist — a lofty, mysterious world, which he will never be able to comprehend completely.

The peculiar feeling with the sense of touch is this: you are so close, you hold it in your hands, and simultaneously it is infinitely distant, more distant than many light years! You experience the sublime greatness of this world through your small microcosm, of which you can only touch the outline. Your own bodily nature, too, remains an eternal riddle. This mysteriousness that always meets you in touch is really typical. If you consider the disciples Thomas and John, you can ask yourself: who was more deeply connected with the Christ Being? One lay at His heart, the other touched His wounds because he doubted. You can think about this for a long time — who was more deeply connected? I don't know. What I do know is that it is tremendous when, like Thomas, you can touch such a profound mystery. Was it sufficient only to lie at His heart? I am not saying 'yes' or 'no'. Here we have come to the kind of ultimate question that seems impenetrable to us ordinary mortals.

That is really what the human sense of touch is: the great teacher of the given fact that we are separate. Separate from what? From the great cosmos. And whether you call it the macrocosm, or nature, or God, or the metaphysical, or the Trinity, I don't care, that is not what matters. What matters is an inner experience of the process by which the sense of touch can reveal itself to us.

I would like to turn to the second of the senses. The term probably implies an unfamiliar concept: **life sense**. What Rudolf Steiner means with this is that we experience our constitution. You have an experience of how you feel. This is spread throughout the entire body. We express this in very simple terms. For instance, when you wake up you notice it. You feel very comfortable, you had a good sleep, and you feel as if you could move mountains. You are probably familiar with this feeling. We are more familiar, however, with that other feeling: not feeling well. Whatever, we have the ability to monitor the condition of our own constitution. This is what is meant by life sense.

The life sense is developed quite differently in different people. A physician knows this only too well. I always give drastic examples, as you will have noticed. There are people who visit me and say: 'Doctor, I do not feel well'. That is not ery unusual for a patient, of course. So, I ask: 'What is the matter?' And he says: 'Well, I just do not feel well'. Then I ask again: 'What do you mean by that?' And he says: 'Well, I feel ill'. 'What do you mean, ill?' 'I feel sick!' As a physician you then have to ask an endless number of questions. You find out nothing. You have to examine the patient very meticulously, and then suddenly he says: 'That's it, there I feel it!' As a doctor you are quite proud, of course, that you have found it.

There is also another kind of patient. They come to see you, and they say, pointing to the region of their heart: 'It is right here, and it spreads out slowly, only to the left, and then around to the right, and then it becomes a little warmer, and it is as if it splits up into three parts'. Such patients can describe their ailment for hours. I could really write books about that − what they experience with their life sense. I am not making fun of it. It is immensely interesting to find out how one person has a clear image, and another sees nothing. The life sense really is a sense with which some people are much more in touch than others; it is more developed in some people than in others.

Now, you can develop this sense in anyone by way of a rather cruel procedure. Because a lot of experiences are fuzzy because of other senses, it is not so simple to experience the life sense separately. But let us put a person in a totally sound-proof room, in the pitch dark − but not this time as a worm, but as an ordinary person, who sees nothing and hears nothing, no sound at all (and there is always some sound, so it has to be a very special room). An absolutely sound-proof and darkened room − this drives a person totally crazy! All of a sudden he starts to notice all kinds of things. He starts hearing the rushing of his blood. He goes "bananas" because of all the things he starts noticing in his constitution.

Fortunately, we do not notice this all that much in normal life, but it becomes apparent that every human being has this sense that is spread out through the entire body. Scientifically we call this the sympathetic and parasympathetic nerves. Everything is permeated by minute nerves, which make the human being aware of his constitution: the life sense. We notice by means of this sense whether we are hungry or thirsty. Yes, how do we know we have to eat, how do we know that the body is asking for food, or that it needs water? For this we thank, indeed, this life sense. You can also call it the *constitutional sense* — the term is unimportant, what counts is that you associate something with it.

We have to ask the question: What is it we are dealing with in regard to this life sense? With hunger and thirst we already get an inkling: we would perish if we did not have our life sense. Imagine that you had to look at the clock in order to find out that you had to eat or that you had to drink something. Would that not be a bit strange? It even goes much further than that. This leads us to a painful aspect of the life sense, namely to *pain* itself. You can understand that without our life sense we could feel no pain either. Pain, really, is nothing but an extreme manifestation of the life sense. Now, in our culture everything is done to eliminate pain as much as possible, for pain, of course, is not pleasant. Still, one might do well to consider all that pain can do for us.

Some time ago — it was in the Sixties, I believe — there was a much talked-about story in the paper, about some people in America who, upon returning home after a short absence, found their young son playing with his fingers in the flame of a candle he had lit. The boy apparently enjoyed the game, for it smelled a lot, and it smoked, and it crackled. You can imagine those parents had a different reaction from the boy's. This was an extreme case of a child in whom for some reason the sense of pain had remained undeveloped. What to do in such a case? Such a child has to be watched constantly. Of course it is terrifying when a child does something like this. But the reality of this can tell us something. What has to happen is that an elaborate supervisory system has to be arranged; when the mother is not watching, the father, or someone else, has to. This child has to be supervised constantly, for the child itself has no *warning system*. Certain people, therefore, have to take care of something that otherwise would be looked after by the child's life sense. From this extreme case we can understand that the life sense is actually a warning system.

You can see it is not such a bad idea that we have our life sense. Because of this, what is happening in our body is kept under constant surveillance. For instance, in cases of something being too acid, or too greasy, or too much, we receive a warning. True enough, the warning often comes too late, but sooner or later it does come. At least, after you have eaten too much cake, for instance, instead of saying: 'My stomach bothers me,' you might say: 'I have given my stomach trouble'. Then you will realize that it is you yourself who in the future can mend your ways. It is very interesting – we would never mend our ways without our life sense.

What would a human being be without pain, really? About this, too, Novalis has spoken beautifully. He said: 'One should be proud of pain. Pain points to the dignity of man'. You can see, Novalis had a different idea about pain from what we are used to in our present society – and Novalis suffered much pain; he died young.

So you see, when we talk about the life sense, we get a new perspective on the problem of pain. What is pain, actually? Why do we have it? As has been stated, it is a warning. But something has to give the warning. Where does this warning come from? This is the question we must ask ourselves. We will have to formulate it quite precisely. The pain warns us that something is not right. That means the warning comes from somewhere where it is known what *is* right. After all, you can only give a warning when you know things are not the way they should be. For a signalman, for example, this is fairly simple, but where is the authority that knows how things should be in our bodies? That is a problem of a different order of magnitude entirely.

Rudolf Steiner gave a name to those powers, those spheres, those beings, who know the secret of our bodily nature. These are of an extremely high rank, of course. For what do we know about our body. Any professor of physiology, although an expert in his field, will acknowledge, if he is also modest enough, that actually we know very little about it. You can read in the papers again and again that we have hardly made any advance in the field of cancer research. We do not *really* know what cancer is. All we can do is note: when *this* happens, then it is likely *that* will happen. But why? That is a big mystery. In earlier times it was said that the human body is the highest creation in all the world, in all of the universe. And in anthroposophy the authority who — to express it rather crudely — has perfect knowledge of the body, is called *spirit man*, in contrast to 'physical man'. This is simply a term to indicate where the power comes from that is able to give us all these warnings. Just think of that beautiful line from Novalis, which points in the same direction.

Man would never be able to develop if he could not feel pain. For pain penetrates all layers of the soul. We learn to find our proper place in the world through this pain. We do not say for nothing: 'You have to burn yourself ten times before...', or 'You fall once, you fall again.' Imagine if you were never allowed to fall. Because of the pain of falling down we learn to walk well, we learn to climb the stairs safely, we learn to keep our distance from dangerous objects. In daily life, therefore, pain is wonderfully efficient in giving us an orientation. This high spirit man sees to it within the bodily sphere that a warning is given. We owe everything to big pains and little pains. It is magnificent how quickly a little child learns everything. A small boy cries when he has hurt his knee while playing games, but the next instant he is back in the game; only, he watches himself a little better. How much 'a little better' is depends on inner maturity. For one person it takes longer than for another. Whatever the case, we can always learn something from pain.

Something else we see more and more often today is that children are much too protected against physical fatigue. They are not supposed to walk too far to school, so they are made to take the bus or brought to school by car. And if the weather is bad we want to protect them even more. However, nothing is actually better for a child than to experience physical tiredness. Of course, children instinctively know this. After too much passivity they suddenly have to run after a ball for an hour and a half straight. Many adults, too, experience something of this nowadays. After a week at a desk , behind the wheel and in front of the television set, many people insist on spending their entire Sunday cutting the grass. This is a far cry from a healthy alternation of physical exertion and relaxation. We really experience less and less that form of tiredness that is so beneficial to the life sense. We primarily know (and unfortunately to an increasing extent this goes for children, too) a different form of fatigue, namely that arising from boredom or from being exposed to too many external impressions. What do you think happens to children who are taken to school by car every morning, instead of walking or bicycling? Do you not think they can hardly fail to become exhausted because of everything they can see flashing by, sitting in the car? I know a teacher who starts the day in class with physical activity before he begins his lesson because otherwise he can hardly get through to the children. This is also something that has to do with the life sense.

We can also learn something else from our life sense. Just ask yourself whether you can learn something from the life sense other than through pain and fatigue. One thing you know for sure: if you had no pain whatsoever, you would accomplish nothing at all. For learning itself is painful. I see how you sit here listening to me with pained expressions written all over your faces, and I am grateful for that, for you would not comprehend anything of what I say if you did not feel at least some pain. You have to exert yourselves. You continuously kill something within yourselves. As you know, it is also impossible in school to learn without the exertion of listening to the teacher and accepting things from him. With discussion and so-called freedom only, you learn nothing. Think about it: why do we have so many narcotics in our time? Could there not be a deep connection between all of these narcotics and this so-called freedom? We want education without pain. When a child asks something, an answer has to be given right away. Never allow the painful situation to arise that the child must wait a while, heaven forbid! And should the child want a treat, it gets one immediately, for it would cause pain if you did not give it to him! That would be inhuman!

Just think it through, the idea that you wanted to bring up a child without pain. You would be starting right away with one kind of narcotic: Think of the way in which fairy-tales are often told to children. How often aren't these fairy-tales edited, for is it not frightening if a child hears a scary story? Isn't the big bad wolf criminal? And that his belly is slit open is altogether gruesome and cruel. The child must not experience pain or anxiety! Everything has to be downy-soft. But the moment the child begins to go its own way a little more, you get the extremes on the other side. This goes hand-in-hand, for a human being wants that other side, too. The great thing about all good folk tales is that these are perfectly matched to the life sense, to the constitution of the child. In every fairy-tale there is a perfect balance between joy and sorrow. A fairy-tale reaches an apotheosis. All of these fearful, thrilling passages in a fairy-tale are quite existential, drastic as the described events may often be. The evil stepmother has to be smashed by the enormous millstone. Isn't that delightful? How else is evil to be destroyed? We do not have to take all this literally. A child never imagines literally what a millstone is like, of course. Whoever claims it does is talking nonsense. The child still enjoys fairy-tales with its constitution. And in this there has to be a balance between the negative and the positive. A fairy-tale is always marvelously composed: relief always comes at the end. The child only gets over the anxiety and excitement in the proper way if the fairy tale is told in its original form, without mincing words, with exactly the same, original words. Even though these sound a bit rough to adults, for a small child the word 'rough' does not even exist. Just as a child has to feel hunger and thirst, so it has to go though the hunger and thirst of the story. This does not mean that we should overdramatize these stories in a sentimental way. It is actually the matter-of-fact way of telling them that makes their images come alive.

What is of importance, though, is that the storyteller has an imtimate relationship to these images.

So, the child starts very early to enter into the life sense. Unfortunately, fewer and fewer mothers have the instinct, the common sense, to recognize that an infant needs crying time. It always alarms me when a mother says: 'We have such a delightful child, it never cries!' That already worries me a great deal. That means something is not right with that child. Of course, it is very sad, this crying, but at the same time you know the child is healthy. You notice this with the delightful sucking noises afterwards.

Because of pain, a human being learns restraint. One learns that one can wait a few more minutes or so. Does one have to sit down at the table immediately, or can one wait for a few more moments? Can one not say a verse or prayer, or does one have to 'dig in' right away? These things go very deep. This constitution sense comes from the highest of spheres, of which it was once known that truth or untruth are quite irrelevant there. These concepts do not yet exist for children either. What meaning has a lie for a child? That is something for much later. 'You always have to tell a child the truth,' many parents say. 'So the stork does not exist, of course.' 'Which stork does not exist?' I always ask. The children are supposed to listen to the mother's belly, for that is where the baby is. You know, I have done a few deliveries in my life. But I have yet to see a child coming out of the mother. Yes, its body does, of course. I have no doubt about that. But who on earth can believe that the child *itself* comes from the mother's body? Can anyone believe such folly? The child does not come out of a body. To the contrary, it has to come *into* a body. And where, then, does that child come from? That riddle has always been answered thus: from an angelic being, a higher being. Now, to a child you can not say 'a higher being', of course, but when we still had a lot of storks, you could point at a stork and say: 'That is where you come from'. This has been forgotten, of course. We have to go abroad to see storks, and then we can see they are indeed like angels when, with their large wings, they soar over cities and valleys. It is a marvellous thing to see. Perhaps you will now understand that this stork story is not so far-fetched after all.

As you see, all of these laws of life have become totally lost. People actually know nothing about life anymore. And this is the great thing about the life sense. It still points out to man how high he ranks. I told you already, in our sense of touch we have left the divine world, but in such a way that we still have a remembrance, a longing to reunite with it. The life sense, on the other hand, which eventually teaches us about pain, gives us the key to the doorway from the soul to that realm where our higher being is at home. You can understand much, indeed, about our age, and its lack of conscience, if you know that many problems are caused by the tendency to equalize everything; no sorrow is allowed to exist, etc. Of course, this then brings about quite a different sort of sorrow. You can seal a kettle when it is under pressure, but the steam will find another way to escape.

The so-called non-authoritarian style of child rearing, too, makes for weak children. Those who always get their way, whose whims are always catered for, will later on be cowed by the smallest challenge.

Here we come back to the question of *narcotics*. That is a kind of pain, too. People who can put up with every-day pain, can also accept the pain of destiny. When one tries in every way to avoid one's destiny, this pain takes a different route, a very sinister route. Then one takes refuge in all kinds of narcotics. In our culture, there is a great battle being fought over our conscience. Will we still make it in this dramatic age, or does conscience have to awaken? For this pain goes so far that it pervades all of nature. St. Paul said: 'Nature, too, craves redemption.' We are not exactly at pains to redeem nature. But if this does not happen, you will eventually see how a tremendous catastrophe will overtake mankind. Exactly the same thing will happen as happens to people when they do not take good care of themselves: they perish, as a result of mistreating their own bodies. This will happen to the macrocosm if man does not treat it with a little more conscience.

Chapter Two

The sense of self-movement and the sense of balance

Today we continue with our study of the senses. Last time we started with the sense of touch. We saw that we never enter into the outside world with touch. On the contrary, we enter into our own bodily nature. Because of touch, we become conscious of our own physical body. This is the opposite of what we experience through the eye. When you look at something, you are never occupied with being conscious of your eye. When you look, you never have the feeling: something is contacting my eye. That is what is typical, however, of the sense of touch. When you touch, you are really stuck within your own bodily nature. I have tried to explain that in our childhood — even from the cradle — we are gradually taught to take our leave from the original cosmic unity in which we existed; bit by bit we define the boundaries of our bodily existence. The peculiar thing is that there is a paradox in the sense of touch. Deep down we never forget that once we were connected with the world, and in the depth of the sense of touch the longing to reconnect with that original world remains alive. That is why the need always remains to express all intimacy through the sense of touch. We keep hoping we will enter this world by means of touch after all, but we always come up against a wall. As you know, you never get through. Actually it is a great illusion when we pet or caress something or someone. Out of this great longing, which dwells at the bottom of the sense of touch, out of this primeval longing, the feeling we have described as the feeling that a divine world exists can arise in the human being reaching adulthood. This feeling we really owe to touch. In other words, if we could not establish our bodily boundaries, we could never have this longing for the divine later on. This makes it clear that with touch we do not observe the outer world, but become aware of our own bodily limits.

It is entirely different with the life sense. This is the sense we use for observation of our constitution, for becoming aware of all our life processes. By means of our life sense we notice whether we feel well or unwell, whether we are tired, whether we are becoming ill, or whether we are hungry or thirsty. All these kinds of awareness are observations of our life processes, which in an abstract way we can call our constitution. In anthroposophy we speak about the complex of life processes rather than use the abstract word 'constitution'. We can also, analogous to Greek, call it the *ether body* of man. What we observe with our life sense is actually the finely articulated etheric life processes in the human being, or at least their activity. Physicians, therefore, are quite grateful for this sense, for it is the signals of the life sense that prompt someone to go and see a doctor.

With the life sense, therefore, we observe our ether body, our life body. We have seen that the extreme form of observation for this sense is pain. We talked in detail about pain, and we have seen that pain is actually meaningful in our culture, in a certain sense. Where pain is avoided, where it is quenched, extinguished, one important thing would never arise: compassion. You could never have compassion for another person if you yourself had not experienced suffering − this would be impossible. That is why every child tumbles down the stairs now and then, and always, subconsciously, wants some suffering as a matter of course. That is why, when a boy plays games, he has to come home with at least five cuts and bruises. Deep down in our soul we know that we could never help another human being in his suffering if we did not continually practise suffering ourselves. A person who has never suffered can simply not be of much help to another person.

It is with the experience of pain that an extremely important impulse has been given to mankind. It is the impulse that produces compassion and conscience. Something very peculiar brought this about. What is it that warns us? This warning must come from an exceedingly high source. Who, 'in God's name', knows when something is awry in the body? And, indeed, this is possible only in God's name, for it has to come from the same source that originated the possibility of the idea of the entire human body. For isn't the body an idea, and not a little factory of some sort, not something put together haphazardly? In anthroposophy the term 'spirit man' is used for this magnificent idea of the human form. Does the human form not have to be a spiritual idea originally? You can not see the human body, strange as that may sound. Only the material shell is what you see. The body really is a tremendously great divine idea, of course. And it is this 'authority', this spirit man, we deviate from when we have pain. We then deviate from the primordial spiritual image of man — that is what we feel. With every kind of pain, we sort of shrink, we lose our 'fullness'. Each pain, or, rather, its origin, derives from our highest state of being, spirit man.

Nowadays we are getting more and more used to astrological terms. Most people know exactly what their sign is, and particularly what the positive qualities of this sign are. Our senses are also related to the signs of the zodiac. But don't imagine that a certain constellation emits a kind of vibration that brings about a certain sense. At the most we can say that certain archetypes appear in the human being. These same archetypes are arranged in a certain order in the signs of the zodiac. Eventually we will see in this course that this order also applies to the senses.

With respect to the sense of touch I have said that the way the human being becomes conscious of himself, of his own bodily nature, by means of the world is a very subtle process. This reflects the principle of the Scales (*libra*, Ω). One knows one is a microcosm relative to a macrocosm. This is how one has to think of Libra: probing the relation of macrocosm to micro-

cosm. This also happens in the sense of touch. Through touch
one becomes conscious of one's own, microcosmic, small,
bounded totality relative to the great cosmos, which one continually bumps into.

The next sign of the zodiac is the Eagle or the Scorpion
(*scorpio* M). The eagle, as you can verify from many sources, is
the highest archetype of man. And the scorpion is the counter-
image, the image of the 'fallen' eagle. We can astrologically
answer the question of what pain is: pain is the shadow cast by
the eagle, which then becomes the scorpion. The extreme
opposites that exist in the zodiac as polarities, such as the fallen
eagle turned scorpion, are always present. The fall can happen
only where something is originally high up. The greatest fall in
the zodiac, accordingly, takes place in the very highest realm.
You also know that the devil was once an angel, a higher being,
whose wings burned up. You can take many more images such
as these. Thus, pain indicates for the human being a 'fall' of
something of the very highest order within him, just as the
scorpion is the shriveled eagle, as it were.

Today we turn to another sense, the *sense of self-movement*.
Here we observe a totally different area. Do not take the sense
of self-movement to mean the ability to move. Certainly, you
can move, you have capacity for movement. You are, however,
also able to notice that you move. When you *see* another
person's movement, you see that the other moves. When you
move your own hand or leg, you do not become aware of this by
looking at it from the outside. You *feel* inside that you are
moving. This is the sense of self-movement. In the scientific
literature this sense is usually referred to as muscle sense.

It is very peculiar that you are not master of your entire body.
If you happen to have a hook-nose, you can not straighten it
just like that. Neither can you stop your heart for a while, or
make your kidneys work a little harder. Just try it! In many
parts of our body we are not in charge. Only in certain areas are
we the boss. I can move my hand from left to right. I can move
my leg. This is possible thanks to the striated muscles, etc. And

all of this is due to the life processes. In any event, part of the body is at our service. And the 'our' is what we perceive. I do, in fact, perceive that I move. I also know it is I who moves. I would get quite a shock if suddenly my arm started to move without my wanting it. This happens occasionally. It is a very unpleasant feeling when your arm moves as a result of a spasm, for instance, and you are not doing it yourself. You can feel it is not your own movement. But as a rule, one has the autonomous use of one's body. One can express oneself, move with one's body. One perceives this, and we call this the self-movement sense or, in short, the movement sense. And this ability to move, this dynamic principle, is called the *astral body* in anthroposophy. Plants do not have an astral body. They can not perform movements. We perceive the astral body when we move. I shall come back to this later.

'Astral' refers to that which is related to the stars (and therefore also the sun). Perhaps I can clarify this for you somewhat in this way: Just as the sun provides energy, and because of its energy makes everything possible, so the astral body is our source of energy. All of a sudden I bring energy into my body. I can pick up this crayon. I can pick up a certain weight, I can expend energy. And we call this energy source the sun body of the human being, the astral body, the star body. It does not matter what term we use. What is important is that it conveys something.

How does this movement come about? Rudolf Steiner once said something very remarkable about the movements of the human being. He said: 'Look, if there is a glass of water over there, and my hand moves in that direction to pick it up, I say as an ordinary person: "My hand moves from me to that glass of water." That is pretty obvious. For a clairvoyant, however, this looks quite different. He would say: "No, this hand does not go from here to there; it goes from that glass of water to me. An invisible hand goes from there to here."'

Now, Rudolf Steiner also maintained, again and again, that we should not simply take on faith everything he said, but that we also have to discover and study things for ourselves. Let us take a nice and clear example, therefore. I have, for instance, a neighbour who lives here in A. I see this man go out every morning and − I followed him quite a few times − he always goes to city B. He does this every day, so I can research this carefully. I have plenty of time to arrange an extensive research project. So, I hire a research staff. We have asked my neighbour whether he is prepared to make himself available, and he is agreeable to this. Every half hour he has to stop for a moment to provide a urine sample so that we can examine his urine. There also is a doctor to take his blood pressure. We study everything about my neighbour, his sweat secretion, his breathing, etc. Everything is extensively examined, for we want to know how he gets from A to B. We have also hired a meteorologist, who measures wind speed, temperature, and the state of the weather. We also have someone knowledgeable in geological processes, so that we can study earth rays and magnetism. We want to know simply everything there is to know about why my neighbour goes from A to B every morning. Well, you are beginning to see what I am getting at. I can study this for years, and undoubtedly come to the most interesting conclusions. I can write volumes about everything I found out about this man going from A to B. Only, there is one thing I will never find out, and that is: why does he go to B? I simply don't know. I will never find out, despite all the data, even if I know his EEGs. Whatever I study, by myself, or with a scientific staff of 100, with the most advanced instrumentation, I will never find out why this man goes from A to B. I would do better to ask one of the people living in his house. And they will give me the answer: 'Oh, B is where his girlfriend lives'. And this is the only correct answer: he goes to B because he is visiting his girlfriend. What is it we are now saying, though? He goes to B because he has planned to go there. He will never get to B if he does not plan to. The plan is already there when he leaves the house. His thoughts, his plans are in B already. Because he plans to go to B, he is already in B. I do not mean physically. No, evidently there is something supersensible. So, from the point of view of this 'planner' in the human being, you do, indeed, start in B. The scientist only sees the body of my neighbour moving from A to B. My neighbour himself, however, is already in B with his thoughts. He is already there *himself*, in fact, and from there he draws his body towards him. This is a common-place occurrence you are all familiar with. My arm, too, gets the glass because the arm is already there. My arm would never reach the glass if I did not have the plan to get the glass. The moment I want that glass, it is already working; my arm only follows the plan that already exists.

We are so little used to reckoning with supersensible facts, and we are so full of them. Just look at the traffic out in the street. Why are all these people driving around? Because they all have a plan — one wants to go to the movies, another wants to visit me, a third wants to visit you. Everyone has a plan, but you can not see this. How is the traffic actually controlled? By all of those plans. When you think about it you start to realize that Rudolf Steiner means that a clairvoyant is also able to see this 'planner', when he changes around the places where the movement starts and where it ends. This is the way it is with everything that has to do with people's movements; you can never explain a movement without including the plan behind it.

Of course, picking up a glass of water, or going from A to B, are only minute parts of a much larger plan, which we call the *life plan*, also called *karma* in anthroposophy. This is the *biography* of the human being. Goethe can also teach us much about this: where we want to understand something in part, we first have to comprehend the larger totality. You must understand: every movement I complete is only a small component of my life. The totality is the course of my life.

What does the course of life really look like? This is the larger movement everybody makes from birth to death. In fact, after your birth you celebrate your first, then your second, and then your third birthday, etc. In your biography you get older all the time, and this continues until at a certain moment you die. One counts from one's birth. When you are asked how old you are, you count from the moment of birth. This is our biography. Can we understand this biography in reverse, however? Can we understand it in the same way as with the man who wants to go from A to B, surrounded by this tremendous research team? Do you understand someone's biography if you start at the beginning? I will try to sketch the following, using an example from Goethe's life.

A certain biographer writes that Goethe was very sensitive, and that this was logical because his mother was very sensitive, and his father as well. Because he was so sensitive and open towards everything he also had this great sense of gratitude with respect to nature. When he is about six or seven years of age, he makes a little altar with pieces of moss and other objects from nature, and lights a candle on this altar by means of a magnifying glass using the morning sun — a very cultic deed for a boy of seven! Fine, then a while later he sees a performance of *Faust* by a marionet theatre that travels from town to town. This makes a deep impression on him, he never forgets it. Later, he goes to university and meets many pretty girls, and he is still thinking about this *Faust*. Well, you see the character of *Gretchen* already appearing. Still later he meets Schiller and Eckhart and all kinds of other interesting people, and he comes across the texts of *Faust*. People say to him: 'Goethe, you have been interested in this for some time, why don't you work it out and write a sequel'. And so we see Goethe's *Faust* appearing quite clearly.

Many biographies are written in this way. What happens to people is explained by what went before. One tries to find the causal connection: what happened to you here sends you there. When you had this experience, you had that experience as a result. In this way one person is supposed to produce something musical and another become a criminal. It is often written so cleverly that as the reader you forget to ask some very simple questions. Are there not thousands of sensitive people, thousands of sensitive children, but very few who build little altars? The marionet performance was seen by millions of children, and yet they did not all write *Faust*. There is not a single student who has not seen pretty girls, but there are not many individuals who have managed the creation of a *Gretchen* character. And all these mighty scholars Goethe met, why, they could have been met by many people. You could read their literature!

You see, it is a bit more complicated than that. And then you get to the big question: How is it that one person goes through life in one way and someone else in another way? In the first place, the things that make an impression on one vary a great deal. For example, two people — they can even be twins — sit in an auditorium or read a book together, and one of them can be totally enthralled by a certain sentence while the same sentence goes entirely unnoticed by the other. Why do certain things impress us, and others not?

When we do not understand something like this we always use a fancy term. We say it is our *disposition*. And yet, there is something to it, that word 'disposition'. What is this disposition, actually? And so you come to the mystery of biography. How is it that one person becomes aware of this or that, while another remains oblivious to it. It does not strike the other as significant. Perhaps one can best express it this way: When you look back on your life, you can categorize it (roughly, for the time being) in two parts: the things you *run into* and the things you *encounter* or *meet*. These are two totally different things. We run into thousands of different things every day, but we only encounter special things. And with these encounters you realize, when you practise a little depth psychology, that they are never really coincidental. Somehow they belong with you. People who want to express it a little more in-depth say: 'It is funny, but when I encounter something it is comparable to recognizing something'. Now we are getting somewhere. You see something you have not seen before, you meet someone you have not met before, you hear some music you have never heard before, and suddenly you feel: 'I know that from somewhere'. How often doesn't it happen that when people meet in life — it does not have to be on the first occasion or the very first minute, sometimes it takes a little longer — they realize: 'We have something to do with each other'. It does not have to be between friends only. You also 'encounter' your enemies. But those are the only people you really encounter:

friends and enemies. In between, everyone is neutral, they have nothing to do with you, they pass you by. Particularly if you have a fight with someone, you can not say: 'That is another karmic stream, that has nothing to do with me'. The one you have a fight with must have something to do with you. That is pretty obvious, for at least something is going on.

When you start working with this intensively you begin to realize that in essence your biography has the same character on a large scale as all these small movements, such as picking up a glass, have on a small scale. Could it not be that there is not only a time stream going from birth to death, but also one going back from death to birth? Would that be so strange? We should say it a little more eloquently: Would it not be possible that we come to this earth with a specific plan? Is that not clearer than 'disposition'? What is disposition, anyway? As if that is something in our chromosomes! Could we not take this as a working hypothesis? Does not every human being come down to this earth with a plan that is quite specific?

Perhaps you know the story of Croesus and Solon. Solon was a wise man and Croesus was a man who owned many camels, much land, and many wives. At a certain moment Croesus meets Solon and says to him: 'I would like you to tell me something. Don't you think that I am a pretty admirable and great man?' Then Solon gives his famous answer: 'I don't know. I can not be a judge of that, just as I can not judge a book before I have read the final page.' Solon, therefore, can not judge Croesus; only when Croesus has died, can Solon judge, only then can he judge what kind of individual Croesus really was, just as you can understand a book only when you have read it to the last page.

In this conversation, the comparison between human life and a book crops up. Just think how a book is written. Let us take a simple example, for instance a mystery novel. A writer of mystery novels starts with the last page, does he not? That is where you find the solution to the crime. The author has to take his cue from this. That is how a mystery story gets written.

Now, not all of human life is a mystery novel, but in some

respects it is. You realize this with respect to some things that are a little more profound. For instance, you find it is clearly the case with artists. A poet is writing poetry. All at once a sentence comes to mind. Then he gets nowhere for a while, but suddenly sentence after sentence comes to him, and at some stage the poem is finished. This gives the poet a very special feeling. When he has written the last sentence, he knows: 'That last sentence is what it was really all about'. Then he also has the feeling that actually everything followed from the last sentence. Every creative artist knows with the last stroke of the pen, when his creation has been completed, that this was what counted.

You will have to get used to the fact in the supersensible world everything runs opposite to everything on the physical plane. Indeed, every biography is a kind of book, and its beginning, its plan, lies at the point where death takes place, or a little before (or after, however you want to express it) and from there runs back in time. Only when you realize this, can you understand someone's life. Only then do you suddenly realize why a Schiller or an Eckhart made such a deep impression on Goethe. And you understand also why in Goethe's youth the marionet theatre made such a deep impression on him. For the first rule of biography is: *The only thing that can make a real impression on you is what you had planned to encounter*. Otherwise it could not make an impression on you; that is totally unthinkable. This is also the way it is with the moment of recognition, this moment when you say: 'Yes, I was actually looking for it, and now I have it in front of me'. Here you see that now we can begin to grasp something of the significance of human movement. Outwardly, it goes from here to there, from here to the glass, from A to B. Inwardly, it is just the other way around. You could not perform a single movement if this 'planner' was not behind it.

We have a biographic plan that lies in the depths of our soul. We do not only have complexes, drives, and frustrations in the depth of our soul, but much else that lives in our subconscious. We have, indeed, a disposition within us. In the depths of our soul we all have our own biography. That this biography is something completed is saying a bit much, but potentially it is present, and our movements take place accordingly. We would not move around on the earth if we did not have this life plan.

Now, don't think that we adults know best what moves to make. Often, children know this much, much better. You could wish with all your heart that your well-brought-up daughter will not associate with that ill-mannered, ill-bred little boy from across the street because he will have a bad influence on her. At a certain moment they do meet anyway, and from then on they are inseparable. You have all had that sort of experience. The encounter between two children is a total mystery. Nobody can ever explain it. It has nothing to do at all with whether or not they are compatible. Children can fight continually, while at the same time they can not do without one another. Until suddenly, from one day to the next, the friendship is over. Or you and your family move elsewhere. You would think the children are very upset. But they quickly forget all about each other. But especially in the life of children, encounters are solid, you can not do a thing about them. There are no options. It is as if a child knows that it has to come on this earth in order to gain a certain life experience through another child. It knows there is one teacher it has to meet, and it has not picked those parents accidentally either.

You might try to look at your life in such a way that everything we now call coincidence actually is an incident that came your way because it was your plan to meet it. At first it is not so difficult for us to do such an exercise, of course, because we first select all the pleasant things. But eventually we start to realize that it was the bitter experiences of life that were the more significant. It was all necessary in order to meet the life plan.

We do not only have our foundation in the life sense, this high being who knows how our body is supposed to function, but we also have the foundation of a biography in the depths of our soul. In anthroposophy, all that is connected with our own sense of self-movement, all that moves us, in fact, all that is biography in us, all that which has a hidden existence within us, is called *life spirit*. This is a very apt term, for you know we use the word 'life' in two ways. Something is alive, a plant is alive, our body is alive — it is permeated by life processes; we live in a natural sense. But we also live in a spiritual sense. If I ask: 'Tell me about your life', I do not mean: 'How is your heart or how are your kidneys?' What I mean is: 'Tell me something from your biography.' We use the word 'life' in the natural sense as well as in the cultural sense. This is the life of this particular person, we say. And the life plan in the depths of our soul is what we call life spirit.

How are all these plans we have individually interconnected? Is my life not inseparably interwoven with that of many others, who have contributed to making me into what I am? In anthroposophy we speak of Christ as the Lord of Destiny. This is all I will say about it for now. For the time being you should only remember the term 'life spirit', the designation for the cultural life pattern of the human being. With this I hope I have made understandable to some extent what the disposition of the human being really is, and that because of this disposition we have encounters with the things around us, because that is our plan.

Now, do not take everything too rigidly. I am not saying that you could not encounter anything you did not plan to encounter. That is not the way it is. We are not here just to follow a program in life. We can certainly also try to get a relation to things that are not up our alley at all, so to speak, things that are alien to our interest. Otherwise we would forever remain within our own, narrow horizon. But you can make a sharp distinction for yourself between the things you have an aptitude for and the things you have no aptitude for. This is already the case in school. That is where you already became aware of your strengths and weaknesses. Fortunately there are still schools where you do not have to start with optional subjects right away. For if a child has to start with electives early on, he will never have to get used to anything new. He does have the need to explore new territory, even though he knows he will never master it, that he has no head for it, that it is

out of his reach. Those of you who have already read something
about this subject matter will know that I am talking about *old
karma* and *new karma*. We have old karma, which we 'recognize',
but we form new karma as well, by developing new interests.
You can easily distinguish this for yourselves: that which comes
to you easily has to do with your disposition, with your life plan,
but those things you have to make your own with great effort
are at least as meaningful for your future. Otherwise you would
be a totally isolated individual.

This is what I wanted to say about this remarkable sense on
account of which we have movement. It is as it were an
intersecting gesture on the physical plane: we move from here
to there, while the 'planners' go from there to here. You can see
that this is clearly related to the Archer (Sagittarius, ♐). Even
though you are not all archers, you all may have to use a weapon
yourselves at some point in time. The first instruction you
receive when you are going to fire a pistol (or bow and arrow,
which is perhaps a bit more elegant) is that you must never have
the feeling that you are shooting from here to there; you have to
have the feeling that you are already in the bull's eye, for only
then will you hit the bull's eye. You have to be out there with
the target. When you are only aiming at it from here, you will
never hit it. You have to feel: my target is over there. Then you
have a much better chance of hitting it. With all aiming
processes you learn that you start from the target, from the
objective. The bullet or the arrow is drawn in from there. This
is the essence of the Archer; when he aims, he sets a goal, an
objective.

Well now, we shall pass on to the next sense, which is
balance. I can see you thinking: 'Ah, I know that sense, that is
familiar to me. I can keep my balance all right!' But you also
have to ask yourself: 'How is this keeping of balance accomp-
lished?' It all seems so simple, but in fact it is all complicated
enough. One thing is for sure: you can only maintain your
balance in a gravitational field. You can not keep your balance
in nothingness. If we were all floating beings we would not be
able to keep our balance so easily. A small child has to learn to

stand up, it must first learn to feel at home on the earth, it needs solid ground to keep its balance. Just as you crawl into your bodily house with your sense of touch, and just as you can experience your body with your life sense, so can you live in that house with your sense of movement (for that is what you do with movement, you live in that house when you make a move). But with the sense of balance you end up in the outer world. You can only keep your balance in relation to something else. You can not keep your balance relative to nothing. There has to be, in fact, an outer world, and it has to be solid earth. In the water it is already pretty difficult to keep your balance. In practice, it is the solid element with which we begin to feel comfortable.

You all know we have an organ for balance. This is that beautiful structure of semi-circular canals, which are at 90 degrees to each other, and which, therefore, represent the three dimensions. When we find ourselves positioned in space, we know what left, right, front, back, up, and down are. These are normal phenomena. How that is related to the cochlea of the ear, how they fit together, I shall discuss when we talk about hearing. I shall leave it out for now. We are now only talking about the three semi-circular canals. The first thing of importance to know about this organ of balance is where exactly it is positioned. We all know that the human being stands and walks in an erect position. I hope that I can make it clear to you that man is supposed to walk in an erect attitude. Let us look at a soldier standing at attention. You can see we can draw a line through this figure: a line that goes through the ankle joint, through the knee joint, over the wrist joint, through the pelvis, through the joint of the upper leg, through the elbow, and through the shoulder joint. Via the jaw joint this line eventually ends up running through the organ of balance. This soldier really stands erect, not more or less. Of course, you can say: 'That is an exaggeration. Normally nobody stands like that.' That is true, but still, we always use this posture as the norm. It is said that someone has a protruding stomach, or slouches, or that he has his nose in the air. With the attitude shown here as a

Organ of balance
Jaw joint

Shoulder joint

Elbow joint

Pelvis/hip joint
Wrist joint

Knee joint

Ankle joint

The erect human being

reference, we notice it when people stand in an abnormal way. We experience that man does indeed stand in a vertical plane, through which we can draw a straight line.

In man, we speak of an unstable equilibrium. The human skull is so constituted that it balances on the trunk. This is not the case for a chimpanzee. The chimpanzee's skull is totally different. Its lower jaw hangs outside its skull, as it were. But perhaps you know that the skull of a baby monkey is quite similar to that of man. When we compare the skull of a baby monkey with that of an adult monkey, it seems incredible that the former, with its similarity to the human skull, could change to the totally different shape of the latter. A young monkey's skull is much more human, with its fine, rounded forehead, which later disappears for the greatest part. Those who can read nature can see that the monkey must have descended from the human being instead of the other way around. The young monkey looks like a shriveled–up little old man. The adult monkey is much further removed from the human appearance. The archetype of man manifests itself in the human figure only. In the animal kingdom it is in principle always lost. You may say that a cockatoo and a penguin also stand erect. But this is not the case. These animals are really completely hunched up.

The ancient Egyptian was much more intelligent in this area.

He said that when a human being had died, he was weighed. In many pictures you can see how the heart and the soul were weighed by Anubis to see whether the deceased's life had been in accordance with his individuality, with his life plan. You can see how a monster eats the soul of the deceased when Anubis determines that there was no balance. In the picture I am showing to you, the human figure of the deceased is itself depicted as the weighscale. It is in balance, so that the monster can be taken away.

From: *From Fetish to God in Ancient Egypt*
by Wallis Budge, London 1934

When we bisect a skull, we can see the well−known base of the skull, and that is where the organ of balance is located, those three semi−circular canals. These, and all the joints mentioned earlier, are in the same plane. You can see that man is like a balance in his human form. And when this is not the case, we say he walks with a stoop or something like that. We take it for granted that this is the way man is. So you can see that balance is the direct expression of our actual being. This being is called the 'I' in anthroposophy — the I of the human being. Indeed, this is the way we experience it. We experience that the human figure is the expression of our I for the very reason that we walk erect. We experience the I as one straight line in the human being. Just as the individual is one I, so his figure is one entity. This we experience in our balance, really. And in this organ of balance the I makes a connection with the world around us.

You can also see this when an infant stands up for the first time. This is always a great triumph. It suddenly starts to experience its own being, and this is something tremendous. Before, he was still a crawling baby. Now, all of a sudden, he has become a real human being, now that he stands up. You experience yourself most intensively when you stand vertically. To stand straight up is to express one's being. It is a pity, therefore, that teenagers —and adults, too — so often hang, or sit, or lie down, for only standing up really expresses the human being. This is, in fact, something that is self—evident, which everyone can experience. And everything that makes standing up straight impossible is experienced as a strong attack on the I. I do not know whether you have had this experience, this I— robbing process you go through when you are seasick. You are really no longer an I. It is horrible, the fact that you can not maintain your balance when you are seasick. You feel awful. You have only one wish: that you were dead. And as soon as you are ashore again, you feel as if reborn. Suddenly you can keep your balance again.

The use of alcohol is an entirely different matter. In that case we actually enjoy tottering. One feels like an exemplary fellow, in total control. But that is not how one is perceived by others. One's flushed face gives the impression of shame, but one has, in fact, no shame left. The most precious possession man has is the richness of his feelings. And it is these that are surreptitiously bemuddled. Spirits impoverish the spirit. You may say: 'Oh, well, but what harm is there in just a little bit, you know, just a social drink!' Right, just a little bit, and you can say just about anything that comes into your head.

But now I come to the question: How do I keep my balance, in this room, for instance? Am I keeping myself upright all by myself? Do I keep my balance from within? Not at all. We keep our balance by means of our environment. It probably sounds funny, but the reason that I can stand up here is that my being fills the entire room. I extend up to the ceiling, over to that curtain, over to the door, to you, to the wall, to the lamp. I fill the entire space of this room. My being is something I have from within, but I throw it out into this space. In the super-sensible world things are quite flexible. When I walk outside under a starry sky (don't be cowed by those millions of light years, our being is not in the least bothered by such distances), my being extends to the trees, to the clouds, and to the stars, while in my room I simply paste myself to the walls of the room. But I always fill the space around me, according to Rudolf Steiner. Now, we have meanwhile become aware that it is not such a strange idea after all that when I carry out a movement, this movement is not made away from me, but towards me. Maybe what Rudolf Steiner said about filling the space around us is not so strange either. Imagine that this is actually true, that I am holding on to myself from outside, from the environment, from the architecture. Can we come to an understanding of certain things as a result? We do, indeed, learn to understand some very simple things.

One of those simple phenomena is fear of heights. What is this fear of heights, really? You walk beside a precipice, and what happens? Why are you suddenly afraid? Why do you suddenly feel this suction of emptiness, and why do you have to step back to hold on to something? Because you have the feeling of being sucked into this emptiness. Why? Because you can not yet fill this space, even though a while ago you still filled the space you were in then. When this stops bothering you, and you look into that valley, what do you actually do? The whole valley is 'filled' with you, and this provides you with support. You are 'leaning' on that stream, on those stones, on that house, and that church tower. You lean on everything, you fill all of that space. And all of us can do this.

There used to be fairs where there were certain attractions that were great fun. They no longer have these. For instance,

there was something that looked like a barn from the outside, but inside it looked like a room, with curtains, doors,
a stove, flowers, etc., all painted on the walls. There were
benches for people to sit on. First there would be a bit of
music, and then, suddenly, the room would move a little –
very slowly, but you could notice it. It felt really odd. Then
the room would start to swing, more and more, and at a
given moment, the whole room would be revolving. And
what did you do? You held onto your bench for dear life,
while everything around you was turning. But the moment
you closed your eyes, it was all right. You were just sitting
motionless on a bench. This was an excellent way to experience how you keep your balance: by feeling the space
around you.

You see what I mean? When the room I was sitting in
started to turn, I felt as if I was the one turning, while in fact
nothing was happening to my body. The moment I closed
my eyes, nothing was happening at all, for I could not see
the room anymore. At these fairs one could experience one's
balance quite clearly.

Now, the peculiar thing about balance is that we are
dealing with the opposite of what occurs with pain. Pain
arises because we turn away from our archetype. It is a
shadow cast by our higher being. We become 'narrower'
than our higher being actually is, and therefore we feel
unhealthy, ill. That is why in the case of the life sense we
are dealing primarily with negative feelings. The life sense
has done its duty satisfactorily when it has warned us that
things are not going well within. Keeping one's balance,
however, gives rise to a sense of comfort. Not to be able to
sit and look around quietly, and fill the space we are in, is
a horrible experience. We have to claim some of that space.
Just as in the awareness of our life sense we experience a
deviation from our archetype, so, when our equilibrium is
disturbed, do we feel we have to recover something of ourselves that we have lost out in the world, as it were. It is a
difficult concept.

Do we all have our own space, or do we have a common space? Actually, we have both. How is it that we have a standpoint of our own? We owe this to our balance. Just try and imagine that you were in a continual flow, like water – that you were in motion constantly. You can imagine that in that case you would never have a standpoint. You could never have an overview. You could never capture that space. To keep one's balance, one always needs some sort of resting point. Of course you can also keep your balance while in motion, for instance while running. But there is always a point of rest somewhere that you can focus on – the horizon, or some other point of reference. The reverse of this is what you experience when you are seasick. You become disoriented, for the horizon starts to move. Normally, you orient yourself in reference to a point at rest, from a feeling of stability in space. This is characteristic of taking a standpoint of your own. And with this standpoint you enter into a space of your own.

What about this common space, then? Imagine that you have all fallen asleep, and that I make a loud noise that wakes you up. A remarkable transition takes place. When you were asleep you were withdrawn in your own world. The moment you wake up, you all enter this same room. Very companionable, although each of you has his own standpoint – on from this bed, someone else from that bed – but, still, you all sit together in one room. This is the case only for human beings. It is impossible in the animal kingdom. Animals never wake up to the same space. You can observe this quite clearly in the zoo, or on the farm, where all kinds of animals intermingle. You can see there that one animal has no interest whatsoever in another animal. Never. You never see a cow tap another cow on the shoulder and moo: 'Hey, look at that delicious, fresh grass!' This does not occur in the animal kingdom. One animal never calls another over to draw its attention to something. And don't say that this is not right because bees, for instance, perform little

dances, after which other bees do exactly what they have to do.
That is something different; that is signaling between animals,
which has to do with instinct. They never take each other over
to some point of interest. You never see an animal that says:
'Hey, look, isn't that fun!'. That just does not happen in the
animal kingdom. It only happens between people, and it has a
deep connection with the organ of balance.

On the one hand, I take a position of my own and I stand in a
certain spot, and yet I am together with a certain group in a
common space. We can really watch each other, take an interest
in each other, speak with each other, follow each other's
thoughts and so on. We are real to each other. This is all related.
You may say that animals are real to each other, too. Absolutely
not. I sometimes express myself somewhat radically and em-
phatically because there is an enormously strong tendency in
our culture to put man and animal on the same level. This has
its convenient side for us, of course, for it means we do not need
any conscience, we can just go ahead and do whatever we like. I
want to emphasize, however, that there are fundamental differ-
ences. I will only mention the simplest of examples. A duckling
gets lost in the pond, it can not find its mother, and swims
around alone. You would think that when another mother duck
swims by she would see this duckling. No way! This mother
duck becomes anxious because that duckling makes funny
noises. This mother duck does not know what to do because she
hears funny noises she does not recognize. This mother duck
does not see another mother duck's young swimming around at
all. You have to understand this. We can meet one another in a
common space, but for animals this is impossible. There is a
beautiful motion picture about animals and people, in which
you see an African gazelle fawn that can not find its mother. A
herd of gazelle comes along, but not a single animal pays any
attention to this little fawn. The animal runs from one mother
to another. It can not find its own mother. It sees the herd, all
right, but only as a 'mass' to flee into, in which to look for its
mother. Think of one of these enormous herds of sheep. A lamb
that has lagged behind 10 yards or so can later on find the teat of

its very own mother in this whole herd without fail. Not because it sees it, but because of its instinct. You follow? Because of the instinct animals have they are driven from within. The lamb is not going to search for this teat, not at all. It just ends up there.

Why is it that only man has this balanced structure? Why is only man a straight line, from which he can determine a standpoint? And why can only man meet other things on his own initiative? On account of his sense of balance. On the one hand it allows him to find this standpoint of his own; and on the other hand it is a spatial sense, which puts us together in a common space.

This is the difficult thing I had to explain today. In anthroposophy, the principle that fills this space, and acts inclusively, because of which we can connect with others in spite of our own standpoint, is called *spirit self*. This is something different from the I. I will try to clarify that with an example. I have already told you how everyone has his own biography, and how everyone also has his own fields of interest, in which he feels at home. When someone feels entirely at home in one thing or another, for instance, mathematics, or history – when he has studied a certain field so thoroughly that he has made it his own, he does so out of his spirit self. This is the great difference between someone who imitates something and someone who has really made something his own. The first is imitation, the second is spirit self.

And when something is entirely your own, it can be passed on to someone else. This sounds paradoxical: that something that is really personal is also valid for someone else. Of course, the angles of a triangle total 180 degrees for all of us, but that is such a bore. What is valid for everyone is boring. What is of interest is what is most personal. This also touches what is personal in someone else. An artist also knows this. An artist can only work out of the personal, and the more personal he is, the more someone else will be touched by him. This is part of the spirit self. Goethe's *Faust* is typically German and typically Goethe. That is why it is for everybody! It is the same with Shakespeare's *Hamlet:* typically English, and typically Shakespeare – for everyone, therefore. There is a great difference, therefore, between the I and the spirit self. We experience the I through the organ of balance, which is the I's foundation. With this we determine our standpoint. But insofar as we fill a space, in such a way that each of us is in touch with another world in a personal manner, we are dealing with the spirit self. It is a difficult concept, but yet one we know from daily life. Which teacher did you like best? Not the one who just rattled off his lesson, but the one who could give it his personal touch. He had made something his own, which implies spirit self. What you have made your own can be passed on to others, and that is the great secret of spirit self. This is the difficult, curious paradox — that we determine our own standpoint and as a consequence we can come into contact with each other. It is not only myself I experience as real when I maintain my balance, but also someone else. Now I am saying it very simply.

Why can I say: 'There is a tree', 'There goes a dog', 'There goes a car'? Because I have a standpoint and yet do not remain with in myself. It is simply that I can see what else there is in a common space. It is all too evident that we have our own standpoint and are still connected with each other in a common space. That is the paradox we express in the spirit self. Spirit self, therefore, has nothing to do with egoism. It is the opposite of egoism, which is why the word 'spirit' is in it. The spirit self is not something egoistic – it is the personal that connects us with the other. That we ourselves have a sense of being, and in addition that we have a sense of the existence of something else, we owe to the organ of balance. I experience my own three dimensions also in my environment.

Perhaps you can see how this is characteristic of the Goat (Capricorn, ♑). Is it not a splendid image, the mountain goat that stands on this totally inaccessible point of rock? I don't know whether you have ever seen the mountain goat. You can also observe an ordinary goat on the farm when it balances on four legs on a narrow spot. Is it not tremendously triumphant, the goat, with all that space around it? Where does this power to stand alone come from? From the entire environment, from all of nature, over which he is, as it were, the overlord.

Chapter Three

Smell and taste

So far we have dealt with four of the twelve senses: touch, life sense, sense of self-movement, and balance. I will briefly recapitulate these for you.

We have taken a remarkable tour, starting with the departure from the cosmic world in the sense of touch. It is an illusion to think that with touch we enter the world. On the contrary, we only become aware of our own bodily nature. In fact, we are taking our leave from unity with the cosmos.

With the life sense we enter our own life processes, our constitution, so that we become aware of how things are with us, whether we are healthy or ill, whether we are hungry or thirsty, whether we are tired, etc. We talked about pain, and demonstrated that pain is tremendously meaningful in the cultural sense, for it always points at the very highest that is present in the human being, even though it warns us only after we have strayed. It has to be an extremely high authority who keeps pointing out that we go astray.

With the sense of self-movement we notice that we have some influence on our physical body. This influence is minimal, but still, we can move certain muscles on our own initiative. There is a potential for movement in our body, and this is what we experience. A very deep connection between all our movements is contained in our biography. In the course of our life as a whole there is always a hidden plan, a plan we have resolved to follow, a task we have set ourselves. We have seen that with respect to this task, time runs in reverse to earthly time; this time starts at the end. The task is not one running from birth to death, but is arranged backwards from death to birth. This plan is also the source of all our encounters. Notice that mysterious concept 'encounter'. On earth we can only encounter that which we planned to encounter. We do not have all kinds of encounters through which we become conscious of something, but we encounter certain things because we planned to experience these things here on earth.

Finally, with the sense of balance, we step out of ourselves again. We re-enter the world, for we can only keep our balance relative to the field of gravitation, relative to something else. I have shown you that the human being is entirely constructed in accordance with the organ of balance, in that our true attitude is an upright, a standing one. To this upright attitude we owe our awareness of existence, our own feeling of 'I exist'. No animal has that feeling. Only the human being can feel that he exists. Only man has I-consciousness. Very curious is the fact that because I exist I simultaneously experience (or can learn to experience) that other things exist also. It is a marvelous expression, this word 'exist'. We do not say only: 'I exist', but also: 'Something else exists'. Obviously, if we were always spinning around, with an ever-changing attitude, we could never face anything directly and point to it, saying: 'There is a tree', or: 'There lies a stone'. This word 'exist' is related to our being, which is an upright being, in an very profound way. We could never say that 'things' exist if we were not upright beings. The peculiar thing is, too, that only man knows about things. Animals never know about things. Don't imagine for one moment that a monkey knows what a banana is, or that a squirrel knows what a chestnut is, or a beechnut. And it does not have to know all this. Its instinct is its 'knowing'. It already carries the connection to these things with it at birth. It never stands apart from them. It knows how to deal with them faultlessly. The duckling does not have to learn where the water starts, and how it has to do its first stroke. The duckling does not see the water. It is one with the water, and it can immediately swim in it. The duckling does not say: 'Here am I, a chick just hatched out of the egg, and here is the water; we both exist, and I am jumping in.' The great thing about instinct in the animal world is that this roundabout way is not necessary. Man, however, is constructed upright in order to become aware of his own stance and of the existence of other things. When we maintain our balance we are not huddling inside ourselves. On the contrary, we fill the space around us — an 'awakening' space that connects us with each other. Strange as it may sound, man *must* fill this space. If he does not succeed in filling it (as with seasickness or fear of heights) he becomes afraid, becomes dizzy, loses the foundation for his existence. Instead of filling the space spiritually with his spirit self, he tries to fill it with something material. In actual fact, with throwing up, you try to do something physically that you should be accomplishing spiritually.

Rudolf Steiner called these four senses the *bodily* or *physical senses* because they give us an insight into, an orientation about, our own physical body. What is characteristic about these four senses, therefore, is that through them we are tied to our body.

We now pass on to four totally different senses. You already have them listed: smell, taste, sight, and the sense of temperature. You will see that these are characteristically the senses with which the human being makes a connection with the world. Now comes the great battle between the human soul and the world. Often you hear it said that here we are dealing typically with the quality of things. There is, indeed, a qualitative aspect to smells, to tastes, and to temperatures. However, what we call qualities are not really the qualities; they are, in fact, sense impressions. Perhaps you will say that hearing also belongs in this category. I will explain to you later that hearing is a fundamentally different kind of sense; it is of a different order from these four senses, which we call the *soul senses*.

We will start with our sense of smell. We can all smell things. We should ask ourselves, though, how this smelling takes place. Now, smelling takes place in quite a different way from, say, touching. When you touch, you come in contact with something and you become conscious of part of yourself. With smell, you have to breathe in. You really have to take in something that was outside of you. No other sense demonstrates as clearly a feeling of *not* dealing with a boundary as smell does. You will never have the feeling: Here I suddenly run into something. Instead, with smell you have the characteristic feeling that you are being overpowered, overwhelmed. This is not surprising. You always have to breathe. You can not say: 'I don't want to smell anything, I will hold my breath for five minutes, or so.' You are forced to smell. You can refrain from touching, but you can not force yourself not to smell. This is typical of smell. It is because you are dependent on breathing, which passes odours on to the bloodstream as well. This compulsive quality is an archetypal characteristic of smell, as it were. When there is an odour, you can not avoid it.

When presently we talk about taste, we will find out that taste is clearly different. An odour always overwhelms you. But what takes place as a result of this overpowering effect? It is as if you have a strong tendency to lose yourself. You have the feeling that you are only a bag that is filled up when you smell something. You never really have the feeling that you smell an odour only in your nose. Yes, when you smell mustard, you can have that feeling. In that case, however, the life sense becomes active, for you do not smell the mustard in your nose, but the mucous membrane in your nose is irritated, and the life sense, through which you also feel pain, plays into it, as it can play into all senses. Just as you can feel pain in your eye or your ear, so you can feel pain in your nose. Mustard actually is something you can hardly smell, but it causes pain and you become aware of this in the mucous membrane of your nose. But if you smell a rose, or another odour (it can also be something nasty), there is something irrevocable, something pervasive, that causes your entire being to be permeated by this odour. This is also because of the stupefying aspect of any odour. You lose some of your consciousness, as it were. You all know that when you enter a space in which all kinds of smells are present, you can not really talk with each other there, or perform mental labour. On the other hand, an amazing thing about human physiology is that we can not smell something for long. After a few minutes in the foulest-smelling room, we do not notice the smell any longer. If someone else enters this room, he has to draw this to your attention by remarking: 'How can you stand the smell!' Only when you leave the room yourself and then go back in, do you notice it again. It is characteristic of the human being, therefore, that the stupefying effect, which apparently is out of place in him, is always neutralized in the organ of smell.

I will now show you how our sense of smell works physiologically. We know that in man the sense of smell is poorly developed, while in animals it is generally well developed. Of course there are exceptions, but, in general, animals have a keenly developed odour determination. You do not have to think only of a dog. It is altogether incomprehensible how well a dog can smell. If there were a dog right here, it would experience a symphony of odours; in a symphony, too, dissonants can occur! It would smell tremendous intervals, probably great melodies, enormous compositions. We simply have no idea what occurs when a dog follows a scent; this is initially incomprehensible. This ability, however, is poorly developed in man. It is, in fact, characteristic that in man the mucous membrane in the nasal cavity, with which he smells, is little developed and only small in area.

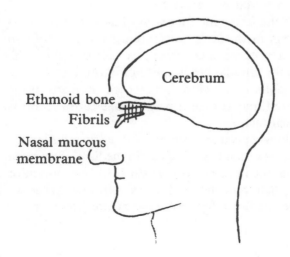

Just take a look at the illustration. You can see the cerebrum (large brain). It is drawn roughly, but it gives you an idea where the ethmoid bone is located in relation to the cerebrum. And you have to visualize that the surface of the nasal mucous membrane consists of a layer of small cells, and that from the nuclei of these cells a fibril grows inward. This fibril passes through the ethmoid bone and goes into the olfactory region of the brain. All you have to remember is that this is a very remarkable kind of skin of mucous tissue, which turns immediately into a nervous system. Nerve hairs, or nerve cells, rather, are directly connected to the brain. Of all senses, the sense of smell has the shortest nerves. Just compare it with the eye; it is a much longer route from the cerebrum to the eye. Or think of the organ of taste; here, too, it is a long way from the brain to the tongue. Or the organ of touch; from the brain to your big toe is a long way to go.

The characteristic thing with respect to odour, therefore, is, as we have seen, that the mucous membrane grows immediately into the brain. This has been shown in the drawing. We can see how the mucous membrane is directly connected with the brain, via the ethmoid bone (I have drawn the ethmoid bone in section). You have to look at it this way: what a dog smells when it walks, sniffing, down the street, immediately 'hits' the brain. The smell enters at the first outpost, as it were, of the brain, which is located a millimetre away from the brain.

Have a look at the following diagrams. The first represents the nervous system of the lower vertebrates. For example, in amphibians, such as frogs and lizards, we can subdivide the brain into forebrain, middle brain, and hind-brain. These run into the medulla oblongata and the spinal cord. In many of the lower animals, the forebrain has a pear-shaped form. In birds it is markedly pear-shaped.

In the second drawing you can immediately see that this is not a lower animal. This is a mammal. You can immediately recognize this by the fact that the forebrain is not pear-like, but consists of two parts. One segment is partly separated from the rest. When we have a pear shape, we know for certain we are dealing with the

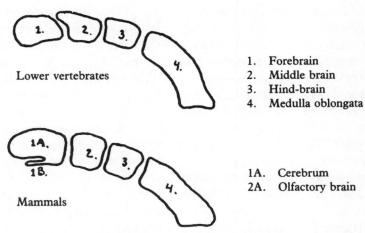

Lower vertebrates

1. Forebrain
2. Middle brain
3. Hind-brain
4. Medulla oblongata

Mammals

1A. Cerebrum
2A. Olfactory brain

brain of a lower animal. All lower animals have a forebrain forming a single unit, even though it may not be all that clearly pear-shaped. In mammals, the olfactory brain is a separate part of the brain. When we compare this for different mammals, we see that in a bear, for instance, this separate part is still fairly large. In the dog it is also sizeable. In monkeys, however, this part is already quite small. When we look at man, we see that this separate part, which has separated off to serve the function of smell, is only a very tiny offshoot. Please notice that only a small offshoot of the brain can be used for smell. You have probably heard that you have all kinds of brain lobes. This offshoot is not a nerve, but a genuine brain lobe, although a shriveled one.

Why is it that in lower animals the brain is structured differently from that of the higher animals, of the mammals? It is because in the lower animals smell plays an enormously important role, so important, in fact, that in the brain it has not separated off. The animal is, in fact, all smell. You know that animals have a very direct connection with the earth, with the world. The organ to which they owe this connection is smell. You can use an = sign: smell = instinct, or instinct = smell, or, to put it more elegantly: *instinct specifically utilizes smell*.

Because of this you will realize that an animal is inseparably

tied to the world, and that it is simply guided by instinct. It is
fantastic what is known about this. Salmon, for instance, return
to exactly the same stream in which they were born, where they
were hatched, because they have an organ of smell. When you
close off their organ of smell, not a single salmon finds its way
back. Imagine! An animal that 'knows' where it was born,
where it was hatched. It has been out to sea, and it knows
exactly how to return to its place of birth via rivers, streams and
brooks. You can only imagine something as grandiose as this
when you take into account the organ of smell. You will say:
'Are there not quite a few animals that can not smell at all? A
chicken, for instance?' Yet, the forebrain of a chicken is pear-
shaped. To clarify this, I will return to the human being for a
moment. We classify people as auditive and visual. Some
people can, as a rule, best remember the things they have seen
right in front of them. A name, too, they can remember better
when they have written it down. Others live more in a world of
tone, a musical world. We always make this distinction. We are
all either 'seers' or 'hearers'. One person tends more to
remembering something he has heard, while another remembers
better what he has seen. Animals live only in the *rhinal*. This is
related to the Greek word for nose — *rhis*. There are 'eye' people
and 'ear' people. There are, however, no 'nose' people, but
there are 'nose' animals. All animals, in fact, are nose animals.
Even a chicken is a nose animal. When it is about to peck at a
grain of corn, it first looks to the left, then to the right, and then
it pecks at the kernel, which is in between the two images. It
does not see the grain; it interprets what it saw as an odour,
whether it is a colour or a form. This is how you have to
visualize it. Animals that do not smell in the outward sense have
to interpret inwardly whatever they see as a smell. That it has to
be this way is apparent from the structure of the brain. Thus
you can understand that the lower an animal is, the more it is
tied to the environment by instinct. When an animal is at a
higher stage of development — and mammals have made a big
leap — the region of the brain used for smell is separated. It is
still large in a dog, in the still higher animals smaller and

smaller, and smallest of all in the monkey. In man it has become minute.

It is known that the higher an animal's development is, the better the animal can be trained. Without much interference from instinct, we can do all kinds of crazy things with them. You know there is plenty of this going on. We are trying to find out more and more about animal behaviour in a variety of situations, and how we can fool them, and things like that. Anyway, science has discovered that the smaller the separated brain segment and the larger the brain itself, the easier you can be fooled. This is nothing new. We have known this about each other all along!

So you can see that there are two opposites: instinct and smell on the one hand, and intellect that has become independent from the cosmos, i.e. knowledge, on the other. This is what the brain is all about — serving the function of relearning what has been forgotten. In lower animals the nose knows all there is to know. In higher animals the nose becomes smaller and smaller. To man, finally, this kind of knowledge has become lost. We have to relearn what was lost with great effort, for which purpose we have received this splendid organ, the forebrain. From this you can understand the immediacy that is so characteristic of smell.

Does instinct have no role to play any more in relation to the human faculty of smell? It certainly does. In fact, it still plays an extremely important role. Have you ever wondered, for instance, why it is that you have become more or less decent people? You owe this to your nose. Of course, your mother often said: 'That's dirty', or: 'That's nice'. An animal never needs to bother with this, but we have to learn these things. And it is a good thing, too, that we do. It is pretty obvious that the principle we call hygiene could never function without our organ of smell. We learn what smells bad and what smells good. If, for instance, you were to take a bath only once a month, certain odours would soon begin to emanate from you that would not exactly be appreciated. This is how odours are meaningful. They are socially meaningful, for if we received no

warning from these odours, we could be in for some unpleasant
surprises. For example, we could get invasions of lice in
schools. If we pay attention to our nose, however, we can save
ourselves a lot of grief. If we have not learned our lesson in
distinguishing what is dirty below, how will we later on be able
to distinguish cleanliness in our clever heads up above?

This faculty of the nose, of the sense of smell, is by and large
quite unconscious. We can, for example, immediately name a
number of different tastes: sour, bitter, salty and sweet. Can we
similarly name any odours? It is very difficult. We can say that
something smells like a carnation, or like a rose, or like cheese.
But we can not give names to the smells themselves. We are so
asleep in our function of smell that we have to resort to
something concrete from the visible world to describe an odour.
We need certain external aids to name odours. We can not do it
in any other way. You can easily make a schematic outline of the
colours of the rainbow. With odours this is impossible. You
have to refer to other things to name them. However, there is
one rough, broad classification we commonly do make: something
smells good or it smells bad. And this is a most important
distinction; it is the basis of hygiene. As soon as we are
overwhelmed by an odour, we make a snap judgement, as it
were, as to whether something is good, or bad, dirty, rotten,
disgusting. Is this not an excellent way to categorize smells?

But hygiene goes much further, still. For the much more
profound, religious concepts of what we call good and bad are
also concealed in our noses. The instinct of the animal is also
based on this. An animal knows exactly what is good or bad for
it. It knows this instinctively — this is nature-bound. For man,
this awareness arises as an impulse out of the function of smell. I
have told you that all senses are great teachers, or, at least, they
can be. We can always be deaf and blind to something. But what
would one say about not paying heed to the sense of smell? I do
not know a word for it — it is such a strange subject area, it is all
so unconscious. From what I related, you can draw the conclusion, however, that smell and odour are the basis, the foundation,
for our *morality*. Without this sense we could never have

moral judgment. This is what is characteristic of odour: it always compels us to make a judgment. And we do this always at a deeper, psychological level of our being. There are very interesting expressions in the language. We say: 'It stinks', meaning it is no good. Is that really so funny? No, there is great wisdom in that. We also say, when something is not quite above board, that we 'smell a rat', meaning that the business has a bad odour. It becomes apparent here, too, that because of the instinctive element in the human being he often invokes smell impressions when he has to make a snap judgment. And what, for instance, do you imagine hell to be like? Yes, it will be dark, and hot, but in any case it will be dirty. Can you imagine the devil scrubbed clean? Wouldn't this be absurd?

When you read Dante's *Inferno*, you almost have to hold your nose going through the first part. And when in Wolfram von Eschenbach's *Parzival* you read the chapters about Amfortas, this wounded king, this king who has to be saved because he has sinned, you read about the stench of his wound. I do not know whether you have read it, but the smell of Amfortas' wound is described extensively. No worldly remedy can drive away this smell, which is the result of Amfortas' sin. Is it not astonishing to read how at one time it was known that morality exudes a definite odour? You can not imagine paradise without the most delightful scents: rose, jasmin, lilac. And does a sanctuary not require the incense of sacred herbs?

There is much to be learned from the Egyptian Book of the Dead. I have already shown that someone who has died is weighed. Following this, the deceased enters the spirit world. He is then approached by the gods. And do you know what they do? They sniff him. The first thing they pass judgment on is his morality. The Egyptians knew this. The hierarchies smell the human being who has died. And that gives him away. No other sense penetrates as directly to the moral quality of a human being as the sense of smell. We have to be very grateful for this sense, therefore, because it reveals to us how things are on earth; we get to know the negative aspects as well. We would never be able to experience the moral quality in life if we had not learned as a child whether something is dirty or wholesome. 'The highest things often come from manure.' This is an ancient alchemist principle. Man's moral contact with the world comes about by way of smell. And especially in our time, when more and more often we have a hard time with morality, we should be developing the sense of smell in many areas. I will return to this later when we will speak about the fact that many senses have to work together. Whether the perfume industry takes moral qualities into account I would not know, but I am afraid not. For it is precisely because smell and instinct have so much to do with each other that there is also a strong interaction between odour and the human being's basic drives. Probably it is this side, which can also have demonic aspects – this is certain – that the perfume industry tries to address first – the basic drives, which include the greater part of sexuality. And yet, however closely smell is related to instinct and drives, we can, particularly because of their moral aspects, train our noses to distinguish true good and evil. Even if you look at a painting, or listen to music, you can learn to smell whether it is dirty or clean.

If I ask you the question where that small piece of mucous membrane we use for smell is located, you all know the answer. It has a particular location in man, namely the nose, whereas in animals it can be somewhere else. Theoretically you could envision it to be elsewhere in man, too, but the fact is, it is located in the nose. Why is it located there? What does the nose express? What is the meaning of a nose for the human being?

Take a look at a monkey in the zoo. You will discover that it is quite depressing to look at monkeys. They always seem to be missing something. They have no nose! Only man has a nose. Did you realize that? Only man has a nose. How many people even realize that this is the case? Is it not great that only man has a nose? Here is something very interesting: In animals, this small brain lobe, the one used for smell, may be separate from the rest of the brain, but the nose is never separate. You can not speak of a nose in animals, for the entire upper structure above the mouth – upper lip and organ of smell – is grown together. The truth is, animals have a snout. Although monkeys have done their best to form a face, they have not succeeded. What does this mean? Why has man succeeded where they failed? In order to explain this, I first have to tell you a little more about the nose.

You know the nose is very human. Everyone has a characteristic nose. Nothing in man is as characteristic as the nose. Actors know this only too well. You can try all you want to change your voice or screw up your face, people still know it is you. If you really want to be unrecognizeable, you only have to use a small piece of plasticine to alter the shape of your nose, and you disappear! The audience does not recognize you. This is very curious. We recognize each other immediately by our noses. There are occasions when we do not want to be recognized, at a carnival, for instance. What do we do? Instead of hiding our ears, or our eyes, we hide our nose. We put on such a large nose that our face is no longer human. Our own nose has to disappear, for our I, our personality, has to vanish. Take a clown. In the early days, this was a condemned person who should have gone to the gallows. He had to put on a white gown, and on his hat he displayed a sign with mocking verses written on it. And he was not allowed to look like a normal human being. What did they do? He was given a large, red nose. For without a human nose, you are not a real human being. You see, this organ of smell we have, which has a certain moral significance, has a very special location. It can only be in the nose, for that is where the human being is really human. The shape of the nose actually changes from the day we are born to the day we die.

Now I have to interject something out of occult science. Because this is an introductory course, I can not explain the following in detail. For the time being, you will have to take it for what it is. For a more detailed explanation I will gladly refer you to the relevant literature.

Originally, we were also primarily an organ of smell. Man once passed through this stage. This situation had to change gradually because we had to get rid of instinct in order to become free beings. This small brain lobe separated from the forebrain and shrank to its present size. In the future everything will be different again for the human being. At present we are in a transition stage, in which the human being loses the old contact with the gods by means of odour and smell, and receives an organ of his own that is tied in with the brain.

What will happen in the future? You can get an idea of this when you pay close attention to the story of Oedipus, who encounters the sphinx, and has to answer the sphinx's question: 'What goes on four legs at first, then on two, and finally on three?' Oedipus immediately replies: 'The human being'. Why? Now, the explanation commonly given is that at first the human being crawls on all fours, then walks erect on two legs, and eventually, when he is old, needs a stick to walk. I can remember when I heard this in school I could not understand why, with such an answer, that sphinx did not plunge into the abyss. I did not understand this, and thought it was a pretty unsatisfactory answer, for mythology was an important subject to me. The explanation was a bit too facile. Now, in Plato you read that for all mythologies there is a popular explanation as well as a much more profound interpretation. So, there is also an esoteric background to the story of Oedipus and the sphinx, for a sphinx does not disappear into the abyss just like that. You can not get the better of a sphinx with a cryptogram answer such as that. For, even though the answer is correct, the actual meaning is much more profound. It is, indeed, the human being who first moved with four limbs. This, however, was in the far-distant past, a time we call the Atlantean era. You can find this also described in detail by Plato. In Atlantean times, the human being 'swam' around with the aid of four limbs. He moved about in a kind of watery situation. When subsequently Atlantis submerged, in many sequential phases, the earth became harder, and solid ground was formed. Because of the formation of solid ground, air was also formed. Man, accordingly, became a breathing being, with lungs that are turned inward. And of his four limbs, two extended down to the earth. The other two were freed for the heavens, as it were, and could be used for work. Man now moves on two limbs, while the animals remind us of the time when we had to move about with the aid of four limbs, even though it was not with the same physical condition as now.

How will this be in the future? In order to clarify this a bit, I will ask you to visualize the head of a predatory animal, of a lion, for instance. It may also be your cat. What do you notice? The lion, and your cat, almost have a nose. When you go and look at the gorillas and other monkeys in the zoo, and you compare their heads with those of predatory animals, you will see that a lion, or a cat, is much more like the human being in appearance than a monkey. Why is this? Because a lion almost has a nose. Of course it is no real nose. Yet, owing to this 'nose', no other animal has such a magnificent expression as these predatory animals. That is why these animals look so human, why it seems they almost have an ensouled human visage. In this we can read something that is related to the future of mankind, namely that the nose has something to do with 'being human'.

I will now show you two pictures. The one on the left depicts the human being as drawn by the alchemists. They have drawn the human figure quite dark, with which they intended to

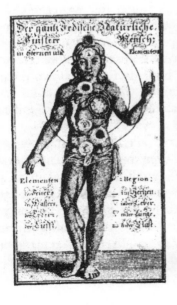

indicate that it depicts the human being shackled to the earth, i.e., earthly man. In the picture on the right you see a different human being. There you see the human being who has risen in the light of Christ: future man. It is very curious: the legs are shown quite dark, as well as the right arm, while the left arm and the head are drawn in a lighter shade. Why is this? In early times it was still known that the right side of man (together with the legs) is the part that is oriented towards the earth, while the left side (including the heart) together with the head, is the cosmic part of man. (In India you can see this when someone is decorated and receives a sash, which is worn over the right shoulder and the left hip.) When in the distant future the earthly, physical part of man disappears (I can only indicate this here — you can read more about it in the esoteric literature) there will be the possibility of something spiritual entering. This is a cosmic law, which also implies the reverse, that where there are too many earthly forces, too much materialism, spirituality can not really penetrate. Thus, where the large 'instinct brain' disappears, space is made for something else. And where our last instinct, that of smell, remains as the last remnant, as the last lobe of the 'instinct brain', man is developing a new organ. This new organ is called the *two-petaled lotus flower*. Although 'place' is a problematic concept with respect to the spiritual (you can not express it in inches), one can say that the two-petaled lotus is formed there where the olfactory brain is disappearing, slowly but surely. This two-petaled lotus is the organ — even right now — with which we can make judgments. With this organ we can distinguish what is significant from what is insignificant.

Imagine the following. You have bought a painting, a magnificent painting, which you enjoy every morning when you wake up. Then, all of a sudden, you lose all interest in it. You ask yourself in desperation what in heaven's name you have bought. You now look at it quite differently. On another occasion you may come across something that seems totally insignificant. For instance, you receive a book from a friend. It seems to be a hopeless book. You put it down immediately, you consider it pure balderdash. At some time or other, when you have nothing else to do, you happen to leaf through that book again. Suddenly you notice a few sentences, and you think: 'Isn't that funny, I never expected to see this here!' You read it through, and the book turns out to be fascinating.

The judgment people have as to the significance of something or other comes about gradually over time. This is often hard to understand for young people. Young people often make snap judgments, while in many cases older people tend to avoid doing this because in their experience the quickest judgment is not always the best. Snap judgments are made with the earthly brain, while judgments made with this future organ still take a while longer.

When we take another look at the picture on the right, we can see that this is an image of the future, in which gradually a mirroring will take place of the Atlantean era. I trust you have gathered that you should not imagine that everything on earth will stay exactly the way it is now. The earth is transitory. It passes through many stages, and the hardened condition of the present will pass. A process of 'softening' has gone on since the ice ages. No one knows why an ice age takes place. In an ice age everything hardens. We now experience the reverse. We are now experiencing a warming trend. The ice is melting, the glaciers are becoming smaller and smaller. You should imagine that in the future everything will become softer and more watery. We will have a mirroring of Atlantis, but in such a way that man will not return to his previous condition, but will have undergone a metamorphosis because of the development he has gone through since Atlantis. To be sure, our organism will change in such a way that once again we will be 'swimming', although not with four limbs. Only our left side will remain, including the head (although in a different form, for the large brain will no longer have any function – the intellect of the present will no longer be of value). The left hand, the cosmic hand, will move back and will be located where the earthly part of our body, our legs, is now. The best way, perhaps, to picture this is to imagine a kind of tail fin. In the future we will swim with our left hand as a fin. That is how we will propel ourselves. But simultaneously, these two petals of the lotus will grow. There will be two new limbs once the human intellect has been overcome. And with these two new limbs we will orientate ourselves in a totally new world. They will be our organ of orientation with respect to good and evil. It will be our inner compass, as it were. Just as now we have a conscience of a kind that arises from the past, from instinct, and from experience, so this new conscience will arise out of our future means of locomotion. This is the human being of the future meant in the story of Oedipus. At first there was Atlantean man with four limbs, and eventually there will be the human being of the future, who experiences a condition in which he has three limbs – the two-petaled lotus and the left arm, moved back as a tailfin.

It is a curious story I have introduced here. But perhaps you can see how all this is related specifically to that part of the human soul that is capable of judging good and evil. This is present in every human being to a greater or lesser extent. In anthroposophy this is called the *consciousness soul*.

I mentioned that today and next week I would deal with the soul senses. We will see that these four senses (smell, taste, vision, and the temperature sense) make specific kinds of judgment through the soul. The sense of smell judges good and evil in the quality of odour. We call the region of the soul through which this is done, this capability of the human being, the consciousness soul. If you study anthroposophy further you will see that we can distinguish certain periods in the development of humanity. At present we live in the period of the consciousness soul. In this period everyone has the task of judging whether something is good or evil at the moment it is experienced; not whether it is correct or incorrect, but whether it is morally justified or not.

This has to do with the whole question of nuclear power plants or of pollution. We can not simply continue to examine with our large brain only whether it works well or not. When we pay attention it will become apparent that everything has a moral value. Then we can ask ourselves whether we are dealing with these things in a moral way or not. This is characteristic of the consciousness soul. Man has to develop a new instinct, acquired through his own efforts — a new organ of smell: the two-petaled lotus. This is what the future depends on. With this, the battle of our time between the moral and the immoral will be fought.

We can see that in our time there are strong attacks. It has always been this way. Whenever something new comes into being there is an immediate attempt to destroy it. The counter-forces are busy destroying people's moral sensibility. You see it everywhere. The highest morality nowadays is what the majority does. In the past it was what the minority practised (morality always arose because a few individuals had a deep insight). At the present time we look for a general opinion about something, and this then becomes the generally acceptable morality. We see this happen with respect to abortion and euthanasia. With this we also see the strong attack made by the counterforces on that new organ that has to develop, which is now available only in germinal form for making moral judgments. Obviously, a moral judgment can never arise in the masses. It is something individual, something for which each one is personally accountable. One can never soothe one's own conscience by saying everybody else does it too. Before the Second World War Jose Ortega y Gasset wrote his prophetic book *Revolt of the Masses* about the average person who only demands rights but recognise no responsibilities. This phenomenon has a fact everywhere. Everyone can experience this for himself.

Everything we have talked about with respect to the organ of smell has to do with the Water-carrier (*Aquarius*, ≈). The nose, odour, *is* man. The entire evolution of humanity is embedded in this organ — from our existence as instinctual beings bound to nature to individuals capable of independent judgment, who have received the capacity for smell as a last remnant of instinct in order to be able to judge between good and evil. The Water-carrier is the image of the evolving human being.

Let us now turn to *taste*. Here we are dealing with an entirely different sense. As I told you, you are forced to smell, for you are dependent on breathing. Your nose is always wide open, unless you pinch it closed with your fingers. Seals can close their nostrils. We can not do that. With your mouth it is different. Your mouth is much more private. It is on the inside. When we want to taste something, a 'door' has to be opened. This is characteristic of tasting. We always have to let something in first. Did you ever stop to think of this? Smell just enters. Taste does not just enter. It is so simple, and yet so enormously meaningful. You can imagine it to be otherwise, but it is as it is, for everything in the human being has some purpose, everything is an expression of something.

Tasting takes place inside. You are never overcome by it. Taste never confronts you with nature in an aggressive way. While odours can immediately call forth certain drives and desires, taste will never do this so directly. We always have to add something. We can do this at the table, or in the kitchen, by heating something, or by soaking it or dissolving it. We can also do this in the mouth; not with everything (you can not taste sand, for instance, because it does not dissolve), but with many things we can do this. Take sugar, for instance. A dry lump of sugar has no taste at all, but when it dissolves it does. What is it dissolved in? It dissolves in our saliva, in something we add ourselves. We have to make an approach to the substance. It is not as it is with the nose, which is only a 'porch', where everything enters freely because it is always open. No, the mouth is much more intimate. Something has to be admitted into it first. Do we not insist on eating with the mouth closed? To eat with one's mouth open is unacceptable, for you relinquish your intimacy. For eating, or tasting, is an intimate matter. You could say, we enter into an intimate conversation with a substance when we taste something. You can not say this of smelling a rose, for instance. We are at the odour's mercy. We 'become rose' entirely. That is not the case with taste. Taste is a two-way conversation with whatever we take in. This is an entirely different realm.

Of course we can approach everything logically. We can say that the mouth is the beginning of the digestive process. As you know, what you taste in your mouth, that with which your mouth has a conversation, is what you eat, what you take in. It becomes part of you. With smell this is different. It does not become part of you. You smell something, and then it is gone again. When we smell a rose, it is 'in' us for only a moment. With taste it is not just a moment. Although one would not say that the tasting itself is prolonged, when we do taste something this has a lasting effect on us. What is this effect? It is that we take in something, something we become, as it were. It takes a little time to consider, to get a taste of, what we will become! First we have to have a serious, quiet, though forceful, conversation, which means eating patiently, chewing well, making an effort. The tongue assists and guards the process. We have to add moisture, and work it over.

To be sure, at the present time we unfortunately often fail to use our organ of taste in this way at all. Indeed, no sense is as degenerate as our taste. It started long ago, in paradise. Imagine the temptation in paradise taking place by means of smell or by means of, let us say, a nice picture of the serpent. Impossible! The serpent *had* to intervene by means of the sense of taste, for if he could lay hold of man there, he would have him. It is, indeed, the faculty we no longer know how to use at all.

If I ask you how something tastes, you say 'good', meaning delicious, or 'terrible'. This is the answer you give, and that is what the Fall is all about. You can have long discussions with people about the reality of the Fall of Man. But there is only one possible conclusion: Of course the Fall is real! Do we not taste whether something is 'good' or 'terrible'? But is that really what creation intended — that we can tell whether something tastes good or bad? Is that really what matters? Hardly! No, what you should be aware of is that when you taste something you take in a piece of the macrocosm, and you have to realize that this will become the substance of your body — the instrument with which you have to go to work in the cosmos. By tasting you have to ascertain that the food is compatible with this instrument.

This is not how it has turned out at all. Or hardly, for I can give you at least one consolation: someone who eats hors d'oeuvres for months on end will end up simply dying for an ordinary cheese sandwich and a glass of water. That is quite touching, is it not! For even though man is a slow learner, he *can* learn something. When you have eaten the wrong things for an extended period of time, a primeval desire for something wholesome arises. Water and a piece of cheese then taste delicious, and you say to yourself: 'It never tasted so good!' Unfortunately, the temptations are many. The culinary art, the eighth of the arts, offers the greatest contribution to a paradise on earth.

So there are certain moments when at least we begin to taste again. This also happens after an illness. For a time one had not been allowed to to eat anything, and then one has a first bowl of soup. What does one taste? Well, something quite different from 'delicious'. One can taste whether it is wholesome or not. These are the only two qualities, the only criteria for taste: whether something is wholesome or unwholesome.

On the whole we have pretty well lost this kind of taste sense. This loss begins in our early youth with candy. We have to try to restore the organ of taste so that instead of noticing whether something is delicious or not, we taste whether it is wholesome or not. At the same time there will have to be a new dietary science. This should not be a matter of tables in which you can look up everything about quantities of vitamins and carbo-hydrates. What matters is the development of our own organ. That is something that would be useful to us and would come from ourselves, and not from some outside authority. And the only question that counts in the development of this new sense of taste is: Is it wholesome or unwholesome? If one can answer that, one can also get a pretty good idea of what one's diet should be. This has to do with quantity as well as quality. For you can learn to taste how much you should eat. The late Dr. F.W. Zeylmans van Emmichoven (1893–1961), a physician and psychiatrist, who was the first chairman of the Anthropo-sophical Society in the Netherlands (from 1923 to 1961), always said: 'You know exactly the mouthful you still need, and the next mouthful you don't need'. I always call this 'Zeylmans's mouthful'. In any event, one really starts to assess by means of taste: 'How much do I need', 'How much liquid should I have with my meal', etc. Fortunately, most people know by now that you have to chew slowly and thoroughly; not shovelling it in, washing it down, as still is the case with spoiled, and, therefore, neglected, children.

In early times, medicines were always discovered by means of taste. The first herb gatherers went off into nature, and the taste of each plant told them whether it would have an effect on the liver, on the kidneys, or on the eyes. This kind of judgment by means of taste should once again be our teacher in taking care of our health.

In anthroposophy, the soul realm that enables us to use our intelligence is called the *intellectual* or *mind soul*. The essence of what is meant here is hard to grasp because we have almost lost the capacity in question. When, however, you think of the term 'common sense' you are coming close. We often confuse intelligence with intellect. But intellect has often become entirely separated from intelligent common sense. At heart, however, we still know what common sense is. Now and then it comes to the surface. It is that by which we discern whether something is senseless or has meaning. This capacity is called the intellectual/ mind soul. This, as I said, has nothing to do with intellect, but neither is it only a feeling; feelings are, so to speak, too subconscious, too dreamy. This 'common-sense soul' lives between dreaming and waking. It is the core of the human being, the last remainder of paradise within us, the last compass that tells us: 'This is healthy' or 'This is unhealthy'.

We can categorize taste to some extent. We speak of salty, sour, sweet, and bitter. Contrary to what you read in books, you can check quite simply yourself where on the tongue you taste something. Take a bit of salt, sugar, lemon juice or ground coffee on the tip of the tongue (rinse with water in between). You will notice that the four main tastes can be quite clearly distinguished here. Try the sides of the tongue (use a small painting brush and a mirror): You will notice that this works quite well, too, especially with salt and sour. At the back of the tongue, a bitter taste is most noticeable, and salt, sour and sweet not so much. The middle of the tongue has no sense of taste.

While a sweet taste satisfies our immediate desire for egoistic wellbeing, a sour taste awakens something in us. It is not for nothing that we give sweet-tasting things to small children first, and sour things only later. Salt, however, wakes you up strongly. Good cooks know this. One has to add just enough salt to a dish to reveal the taste concealed in it. Salt should not work on its own. While sweet and sour are tastes by themselves, it is the task of salt to enhance other tastes. When you eat an egg on its own, it has hardly any taste at all; with salt it tastes much better. This is really quite a mystery.

Salt is connected with thinking. Thinking is never really directed at itself, but always at something else. When I regard a dandelion and then communicate my thoughts about this dandelion, I am not speaking about the thoughts, but about the dandelion. And if I do it well, you will know eventually what a dandelion is like. When suddenly you see this dandelion in front of you, I have 'sprinkled salt' on it. Thinking explains something outside itself; it forgets itself.

Bitterness, finally, always represents a kind of victory for the will. You always have to engage the will to cope with bitterness. That is why small children never like to eat bitter things, and when they are a little older will tell you proudly: 'I like chicory now'. They have matured somewhat when they can stand that. Indeed, one has to be able to manage bitter pills. The same thing emerges here as it did in connection with the life sense. We could never feel human without pain, without the bitter aspects of life, without having to exert ourselves for something. This engages our will. If you give your child only sweets, and not something bitter once in a while, it will never be a vigorous child. Our entire psychology, therefore, is connected with our nutrition. In summary: 1. salt: basis for awakened consciousness; 2. sour: refreshing, activating; 3. sweet: general sense of wellbeing; 4. bitter: resistance for the will.

Another aspect of nutrition is quality. How does quality come about? You know how much wisdom there is in the language. We all know what it means when we say someone has good taste. We do not mean that this person knows exactly what a hamburger should taste like. No, we mean that this person knows how to dress well, that his or her room, or house, is attractively decorated, etc. It is really curious that for a totally different thing we use the expression 'good taste'. Where does this come from?

I have related that when we taste something we are on that boundary where a substance from the outside world is about to become inside world — in other words, will become an assimilated substance of our own. What is it really that we taste? What we taste is whether it agrees with us, whether it is wholesome or unwholesome. And what is the essence of this food, about which we want to know all this? It is what nourishes us. You could, perhaps, compare it with a kind of fertilization process. What we actually do is to taste how the world will fertilize us and whether or not this agrees with us. There are interesting ancient Egyptian pictures of how a pharaoh drinks from the udder of a heavenly cow. What we really taste is the instant of transition, in which the world starts to form us.

And what do I do when I dress in a certain way? When I decorate my room? What am I really doing? I am fertilizing the world! There is not only the cosmos nourishing us, caring for us, and protecting us. We have a response, a rejoinder, a counter action. This is our *culture*. When we speak about culture, we always refer to taste in this connection. Has something been tastefully decorated? So on the one hand the cosmos provides us with substances we take in and taste on the boundary; and on the other hand we give something to the world by means of exactly the same process, which is why we use exactly the same word: taste. Just as the world dresses us up, so we dress up the world, as it were. To put it more seriously: Just as the world transforms us from macrocosmic substance to microcosmic substance, so do we change the world, imprint our own stamp on it. This is what is meant with this use of the word taste.

You can see that taste goes much deeper than smell.

When, for instance, you look in the bible for the most striking parables, which do you look for? Which are the most expressive parables? They are the parables of hunger and thirst. When you want to express something really profound, you do this in terms of hunger and thirst — something that seems so mundane. But eating is really a sacred affair, just as the formation of culture is a sacred matter. The first is the fertilization of man by the world, the second that of the world by man.

The fructification of man by the world goes way beyond the ingestion of food. This is only the first stage of the fructification process. I said already that there is much wisdom hidden in language. There is much in the language that can make it clear what else there is that has to do with the fructification of man by the world. We talked about nourishment. We also speak of spiritual nourishment. We spoke about ingesting substance. We also know about substantial ideas. Not only can food be indigestible, but a book or a lecture can be as well. In essence, we make no distinction between spiritual and earthly food. In essence it is the same. I feel this is expressed beautifully in the verse of Angelus Silesius: 'Mere bread can not sustain us; — The healing it does give — Is God's eternal Word, — Is Spirit, and is Life.'

It is an illusion to think that atoms, or substances, could heal us. We are always healed by means of fructification processes. And this can be a bitter experience. Is it not peculiar how life experiences, the trials of life, are also expressed in terms of taste? 'A bitter experience.' 'A sourpuss.' 'A sweet child.' It is quite interesting that in ancient Egypt, where the greater part of the culture took its course in boats along the Nile, a single word meant 'boat', 'life experience', and 'taste'. This is amazing — the same word for the boat on the Nile, the taste on one's tongue, and the life experiences one meets through one's **destiny**. This destiny, in fact, is the highest form of fructification for man. With all the trials and tribulations you meet, you might well ask yourself: 'Is this not part of my nourishment? Can I not also, or actually, draw a tremendous healing force from the most tragic and dreadful experiences?' As you know, the greatest healing forces are in bitter substances. Would we not be much stronger, much healthier, as a result of disagreeable experiences?

This is what I wanted to say about taste. And you will understand that with respect to taste we have to do with the zodiacal sign of the Fishes (*Pisces*, ⋊). The Fishes is the Christian sign of the zodiac, for Christ is the Lord of healing. The Fishes has to do with the healing element in the world. You all know the biblical story of Tobias, which makes this quite clear. It is not for nought, therefore, that in bio-dynamic agriculture the healthgiving aspect of the earth is primary. This involves seeking the truly Christian healing forces in the earth, the ones that are truly health-giving. Of course it is nice when food is also tasty, and not so nice when it is wormy. But is this the most important thing? Whether it will in the end save humanity if this is all we take notice of is what I wanted to talk about this evening. What matters is whether we have enough life force to spare; and whether we give the being who fructifies our destiny, who helps us in the forming of our destiny, a chance. That is our task: to build up a Christian culture. And this is a matter of good taste. From this point of view it would be good not to speak of 'natural' food. We hardly eat any natural food. Only animals do. We eat 'cultural' food. For agriculture is a *culture*. The only question we should ask in agriculture is whether we pursue a healthy culture or a pernicious culture. The result of a healthy culture is 'healthy cultural food', from which we can prepare the dishes that feed us. We do not eat abstract proteins, carbohydrates, fats, and minerals. We eat prepared meals. We still owe everything to ancient cultures – our grains, and many fruits, to Persia, our cabbage to Egypt, etc. We owe this to the dedication and wisdom by which they succeeded in bringing the fructifying forces of the sun into the earth.

Moreover, we eat at the table, together with others. Having always to eat alone is unhealthy. The dishes are prepared. It is to be hoped that we, too, are equally tastefully prepared. The meal is served in serving dishes, and put on our plates. We eat with 'instruments'.

There is a vast difference between an apple thrown on the table, and one served on a dish. Our uncultic society has great difficulty in understanding this. Just as we no longer experience the meaning of the priest standing to the right or to the left of the altar, or of the book being open or closed. What is there in a gesture? What is the gesture of a certain garment?

Our mouth is an inner room. It is best, therefore, to eat inside. I hope I do not insult campers. Enter a room to sit down at the table, and three cultural experiences come together: 1. for our bodies, from the past, the preparation of the food; 2. for our soul, here and now, the arrangement of the room, the table, the lighting, our dress, our behaviour; and 3. for the spirit, fructifying the future, our conversation about our experiences.

This could be a blessed, all-embracing rhythm indeed.

Chapter Four

Sight and the temperature sense

We are now in the middle of this series of lectures, and by now you will have discovered that it does not make much sense to talk about nerve stimuli. We are used to saying of an impression of smell that it is a nerve stimulus of the nasal mucous membrane. Well, we can say of anything that it is a nerve stimulus. Except that there is one thing that can never be stimulated, and that is a nerve. You will never, in your whole life, manage to stimulate a nerve. It is impossible. You can at the most stimulate a person. You can, indeed, say that the human being has certain experiences for which he needs nerves, and that he is stimulated thereby. But that is such a generalized, meaningless way of putting it. What I am trying to do is to ascertain what particular kind of stimulus we are talking about, and what is behind it. And by now you will have become aware that the various categories differ from one another a great deal. The sense of smell is fundamentally different from the sense of taste. I hope that it has become more or less clear that, in the realm of odour, we always make a judgment when we smell something − a moral judgment, in fact. We can always smell it whether something is tainted or is all right. All concepts of good and evil that may arise in the human being at a later age have their origin in this judgment of whether something smells spoiled, bad, evil, or nasty, or whether something has the scent of holiness about it (think of incense!). We are forced to smell because of that nose. It is simply there, and we are forced to breathe through it. I have shown that this involves the shortest nerves −

that the brain is almost immediately 'touched'. You can experience this. You are stupefied by it, overwhelmed. You can do nothing about it. And if you can not stand someone, you can barely look him in the face without showing your dislike. We react immediately to this sort of thing. This is the typical thing about odour. It enters, and we react. We have the greatest difficulty interposing our humanity. There is hardly time.

Taste is much more intimate. There is plenty of time. Everything takes place in the intimacy of one's inner world. We have to go to the trouble of opening our mouths ourselves. We always have a say in relation to taste, which is not the case with smell. Taste is a much more intimate process. The taste nerves are longer, too. With taste one is on the very threshold where outer world becomes inner world. By means of taste one checks whether the substance to be absorbed can become a healthy substance for one's own microcosmic bodily nature. It is actually a sort of fructification process. I had to give voice to the gloomy thought that no other sense is so misused, that taste has nothing to do with tasty or not tasty, but that in essence through taste one ought to get an idea of what is healthy and what is unhealthy. This is really what we should be tasting with our organ of taste. I drew your attention to the Fall of Man, and how taste is related to it, and also how there is healing power in the organ of taste. All religions have always known that, ultimately, everything is substance, whether it is earthly food or spiritual food, and that healing has to take place by way of the mouth. This is related, of course, to the sacrament of communion, for this makes use of a substance to heal the human being. In reverse we can say: Even when one only prays or meditates ('only' is already a lot!), one has to be so concrete that one 'tastes' one's prayer or meditation. Rudolf Steiner indicated that when one reads a verse, or something else of importance, or when one says a prayer, one should not merely mumble. In earlier times people never prayed in an abstract way, with the head. One always recited the text because it had to be 'tasted'. (A left-over from this is mumbling; you notice this with priests when they read their breviary.) Also, when a meditation is handled concretely, it should be as concrete as when eating a ham sandwich, for instance. Only then do you become aware of how great a healing force this contains for the future of mankind. We have to learn to deal so concretely with spiritual matters that we become aware that this is what really constitutes concrete 'nourishment'. We have to learn again to 'taste' this aspect.

We have also seen that the human being has an outward taste, with which he forms the culture of the time. This involves the same process as the fructification of the human being by substances. The world is fructified by man in that culture is formed. We have spoken of human destiny, which also contains every kind of taste — bitterness, sourness, saltiness, and sweetness. This, too, is a fructification process for man: the destiny he is bound to undergo. For a bitter destiny can be quite important for the human being in its healing power. This does not apply to the individual only, but also to the culture as a whole. For do we not often see how an entire culture degenerates when all the the 'good things of life' are too freely obtainable?

We now pass on to an entirely different sense, namely of the eye — human sight. The human eye is a quite exceptional sense organ. Most senses, you see, are created somewhere on the surface of the human physique. We have seen this to be the case for smell, where a certain surface area becomes sensitive, so to speak, and somehow becomes connected with the brain. It is the same with taste; somewhere in the mucous membrane of the tongue an array of tiny cups is created, which become connected to the brain. We will see later on that the ear, too, was created out of the skin. The principle of these senses is that a small section of surface becomes sensitive in a specific way, and subsequently becomes connected with the brain.

The eye goes against all these rules. This is something quite miraculous, which was discovered in embryology. For the eye, the formative process goes the other way. Instead of something at the surface becoming sensitive and connecting with the brain, the eye starts with the brain itself. Let me put it this way: The brain becomes 'curious'. It starts to extrude. Unfortunately, our brain can not grow when we have become adults, but in the embryonic stage everything is still full of growth — very mobile and flexible. Everything is undergoing continuous change. In the embryonic phase something very curious takes place during the growth of the brain. It grows outwards in two protrusions and forms two cups that grow towards the skin. And then the skin starts to do something, too. It starts to grow inwards. The skin meets the process of the formation of the two cups with the formation of two lenses. Something is created from out of the skin, therefore, but these are only the lenses. With the lenses one can not see. One sees with the sensitive retina behind the lenses.

It is amazing to realize that when an optometrist looks through the pupil into the eye with his small mirror, he is looking directly at the brain, at this protrusion. You may have heard about the three membranes around the brain: on the outside the tough dura mater, the arachnoid membrane in the middle, and

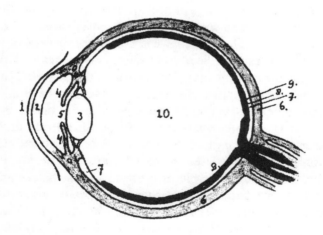

1. Conjunctiva	6. Sclerotic coat
2. Cornea	7. Choroid coat
3. Lens	8. Pigment
4. Iris	9. Retina
5. Pupil	10. Vitreous humour

Section of the eye

the pia mater on the inside. With the formation of the eyes, these three membranes extrude along with the brain. Now, the white of the eye corresponds exactly with the dura mater of the brain. When you look at the white of the eye, therefore, you are looking at the 'extension' of what envelops the brain. You also encounter the arachnoid membrane in the eye, as the choroid coat behind the nerves. This membrane provides nourishment to the eye, just as the cerebral cortex has to be nourished. It is indeed quite amazing that the brain itself goes ahead and, against all the rules, forms a sense organ.

In the eye, therefore, everything that normally lies concealed in the brain is right out in the open. The brain, while totally enclosed, seeks the light via the eyes. You can observe the same thing quite well in the plant world. What happens when a plant slowly but surely finds its way from the darkness of the earth to the light? The plant flowers. You find exactly the same thing with the human eye. Where the brain has found the light, colours arise, just as with the flowering plant. Actually, the fact that the eyes have a colour serves no useful purpose. You really do not see any better or less well with blue eyes than with gray, green, or brown eyes. From the point of view of utility, eye colour has nothing to do with vision as such. But from a spiritual point of view, the eyes are bound to be coloured because they are involved in the process of going from darkness to light. The colour of our eyes, therefore, is an expression of something, without having any utilitarian purpose.

We speak quite rightly about the iris, for it *is* a rainbow. A rainbow, you see, follows the laws of colour — not those of Newton, but rather those of Goethe; you can not explain the colours of the eye on the basis of electromagnetic vibrations, but you can explain them according to Goethe's colour theory. Goethe has shown how colour arises from the inter-action between light and darkness. According to Newton, all colours are present in light; they are extracted from light by means of prisms, etc. With this, Newton follows the mode of thought that is generally adopted in natural science, namely

that all kinds of things can change as a result of shifts of
atoms or an increase or decrease in vibrations, but something
new can never arise. In Goethe's colour theory, on the other
hand, you find the curious, unusual proposition that colours
are *created*. And we can all observe that colours *are* created.
We only have to learn to look at simple every-day phenomena,
such as, for example, the setting sun. What do we see when
we look at the setting sun, when we look at a darkening of the
light? What we see is that colours arise when the light in the
background is colourless − invisible, therefore − and darkening occurs in the foreground. The invisible light gradually
turns yellow, then orange, then red as a result of the darkening.
And vice versa, when we look at something dark, a dark
mountain, for instance, or at a colourless black sky, and a veil
of light comes from the valley in front of this mountain or
against this night sky, we see a magnificent blue or violet
colour. We can see real violet only if we are very high up in
the mountains, or if we ascend to great height in a balloon.
We then see the sky as blue, while the mountains are beautifully
accentuated in violet.

Goethe puts it this way: There are two possibilities when
light and dark interact. Either light overcomes darkness, and
the active colours arise, with red, orange and yellow hues; or the
element of darkness prevails, creating blue and violet.

Picture a rainbow. You have all seen one at one time or
another. But did you realize that above the rainbow the sky is
darker than below? Just watch the next time you see a rainbow.
It is so clearly visible that many of you will be amazed that you
never noticed that on the red side the sky is darker than on the
blue and violet side.

What has this to do with our eyes? It is not for nothing that we
call the coloured part the iris, the rainbow membrane. For
whatever the colour of your eyes, they are never of a homogeneous
colour. While they do not have the entire spectrum of colour the
rainbow has, there is nevertheless a range of colours from the
black centre, the pupil, to the periphery, adjacent to the white
of the eye. Just look carefully at brown eyes sometime. They are

never entirely brown. When you look someone with brown eyes in the eyes, using a small light, you will see that around the black pupil it is really red, and that the rest of the iris is not plain brown, but that at the edges, where it meets the white of the eye, it tends towards green, or perhaps even very dark blue. It is the same with blue eyes. On the outside we see a greenish tint and on the inside a yellowish tint, and often even a clear yellow border. In other words, the same law that applies to the rainbow applies to the iris: On the dark side, by the pupil, we have the active colours (red, orange, and yellow), and on the other side, by the white of the eye, we have the dark colours (green, blue, and violet). Just remember that with the rainbow it is dark above, and with the eye the middle is dark.

You will never explain this by means of electromagnetic waves. It is only explainable through the laws of nature as interpreted by Goethe, and that is that on the dark side the active colours emerge, and on the light side colours such as green, blue, and violet. You will be surprised that when you look each other in the eyes with the appropriate light source this always holds. Of course, there can be deviations such as smudges or stripes, and even an entire segment can be of a different colour.

Around the normal rainbow, a second rainbow may appear – its colours in a reverse, mirror image. Here, the outside is light, the inside dark, the very same as the eye, therefore. Just as the sun conjures up its image in the millions of raindrops, does it appear in the millions of eye globes. *In the next part of the lecture, Dr. Soesman carried out a number of experiments with colour. In this report, an attempt has been made to describe these experiments in such a way that the results become clear to the reader.*

Another well-known experiment is that the colours can be followed through a complete circle. See, I start with red, this passes into orange, yellow, green, blue and violet, and now this becomes purple, and then we are back again to red. ? This is the miraculous thing about colour. Just try it with sound! You can not play a scale from low to high and come out low again. You will never succeed. Nor can you taste that way. Even temperatures can not get warmer and warmer and eventually come out cold. The great miracle of the eye is that you can go around in a circle. This cannot be explained electromagnetically either. We can say that colour has to do with all kinds of vibrations, which have the effect that there are colours we can see, and others we can not see, such as infrared, which we can feel, and ultraviolet, but this has nothing to do with understanding it. This never explains why colours can be arranged in a self-contained circle. And yet, this is the case. You can clearly observe in the phenomena that colours are a self-contained totality. We can trace them through a circle.

We also know that when we look at one colour for some time, we suddenly seem to see another colour when we close our eyes or look the other way. This is always the colour opposite the observed colour in the colour circle, which arises as a result of a process in the human soul. This only happens with colour. Imagine, when you taste something sour, a sweet taste emerging on the other side of the tongue! It is unthinkable. Or imagine smelling a sewer and at the same time an impression arising of the sweet scent of a lily! The miraculous mystery of the eye, which we can not emphasize enough, is that it is able to complement harmoniously what is missing.

A most peculiar experiment, which clearly demonstrates the totalizing capability of the eye, is the following: Here you look at three vertical panels side by side of equal width. The two outside panels are bright orange, and the one in the middle gray. Try and fix your gaze on them for a minute or so. In the middle of the gray panel is a black dot you should look at, in order to prevent eye movement as much as possible.

Now I remove the display. Look straight at the softly lit screen: what you see now is orange instead of gray in the middle, while the previously orange panels are now blue – the opposite colour. Remember, the neutral gray area now also appears in colour. This experiment designed by Goethe demonstrates vividly that the entire eye becomes colour-active. Please, remember this experiment as long as you live!

Better known are the experiments with coloured shadows. Two projectors, one with purple light and the other with ordinary white light, produce two shadows of the pillar placed in front of the screen. One shadow is purple, as you would expect, and the other has the opposite colour: green! The eye always complements. Purple calls up green. Similarly, red light calls up blue, as you can see, and yellow light produces a violet shadow.

It is not sufficiently well known that purple makes the colour green appear, and red the colour blue. When I show purple and red on the screen side by side (with a single projector, without the pillar), let you stare at a black point on the borderline for a minute or so, and remove the image, you see green where it was purple before, and blue where it was red!.

Having done these experiments, I want to return to the question of what colours are. Try and imagine the following. You have never before in your life seen colour. All your life you have gone around in a moonscape. In a moonscape one does not really see colour. For the moment you have to forget everything that has to do with colour, and imagine that all your life you have been in a black-gray-whitish environment. Next, imagine that you start seeing things in colour for the first time in your life. What would happen to you inwardly? We are so used to colour that it is hard to imagine this. I am convinced something overwhelming would happen to you inwardly. It would be as if you had just entered a tremendous exhibition. It would be an enormous transition. It is difficult to explain this clearly, but I hope you get an idea. What we experience when colour is revealed is that the inner essence of nature appears. As long as you see only gray and black and white, you are really only looking at the outside surface of things. Their inner being does not show itself — nature hides itself. But when colour appears, the secret of nature emerges. Perhaps this is comprehensible if you think of a garden with only green, where all at once, on a sunny morning, a multitude of flowers bloom. I mentioned before that only in the flower does the secret of vegetation become apparent. As a result of the appearance of colour, nature, in a mighty exhibition, displays its inner workings to the outer world. This is the secret of colour.

Because we are always locked away within the human soul, within ourselves, we always want to open ourselves to nature. But in no other of the senses does nature reach out to us to such an extent, and this is because the cosmos comes to our aid: No sun, no sight! For just as our inner sun wants to illuminate something, so a sun in the universe is required to reveal to us this overwhelming exhibition of nature.

What happens when you look at a colour? What is the most elementary thing that happens in your soul? First I will say it quite simply: You become involved. And with this I mean that suddenly a new element is released in the human soul, for which we do not have a word. How do you experience colour? I still find the best word is *mood*. It is terribly difficult to express a mood in black, white, and gray. However magnificent in composition a drawing or an etching may be — however moving, for instance, the black-and-white drawings of Rembrandt — the real mood only appears with colour. Perhaps you can yourselves find a better word to express this. What I wish to indicate with the word 'mood' will perhaps become clear if I give a few examples. Take the colour yellow. You can not say of it: 'Good heavens, what a gloomy yellow!'. That is impossible, isn't it! Nor can you say: 'What an exuberant violet!' It is just as impossible. Or: 'What a limp red!' We can not be talking about red! With colours you immediately experience an emotion. The most elementary things slumbering in the soul make their appearance.

Is it not terribly interesting that we speak of the human visage? We do not mean vision, but the entire human face. We do not say someone has interesting hearing; no, we speak of an interesting visage. The eyes are so centrally located, they are so expressive, so colourful, so 'flowering', that we name the entire face after them. It is not so strange, therefore, that they are located in the very middle of the face. Of course, they could have been situated elsewhere, for instance on top of the head. That would have been much more convenient, perhaps. That is maybe where we ourselves would have placed them. But, no, they are right in the middle, simply because we *have* a face, and because the human soul expresses itself in the face. We rarely fall in love through the ears, or the nose. It is possible, no doubt, but not so likely. We meet directly soul-to-soul via the eye. The eye really is our mirror, the direct representation of the human soul. We also cry and look happy with our eyes, for that is where we encounter the most elementary emotions. Because of beautiful music we can get tears in our eyes, but we do not get runny ears!.

And yet, this is only one aspect of the human eye. For there is something else. Just take a look at the illustrations. On one you see a black vase. Or do you see two white faces? You become confused. With some practice you can play with this. One moment you see it this way, and the next moment the other way. This is because you have 'supersensible arms', which grasp the picture now this way and now the other.

In the other illustration you see an inward spiral. But is it a spiral? What do you find when you trace the lines? They are, in fact, the most perfect circles you could imagine. There are hundreds of tricks like this, which we call *optical illusions*. It is too bad, but our eyes can be fooled. You will not succeed in fooling the other senses the same way. You can persuade a child to take a bitter pill by coating it with sugar, but if he chews on it for too long it will be bitter all right. You can not fool taste. But the eye is gullible. You can look at the illustration for as long as you want, but you will not succeed in seeing circles instead of a

spiral. How is it that we can be so mistaken in the use of our eyes? It is because we 'think in our eyes'. This is why animals in nature are never mistaken. As soon as animals associate with people, they can start doing funny things and making mistakes, but in nature an animal never makes a mistake — because it never thinks. Only man thinks about things, and because thinking occurs especially in association with the eye, illusions are possible only through the eye. With our thinking we add what we expect to see to what we actually do see, and as a result we have optical illusions. It might be better to speak of illusory insight.

This is the other side of the eye. On the one hand it is an emotional sense, and on the other hand a scientific instrument.

We have been dealing with a number of senses. Why are we able to talk about them? Because we have studied them by means of the eye. We can not speak about the eye by means of smell, but we can talk about smell by means of vision. The eye is the sense organ that contains all other sense abilities. We keep our balance by means of our eyes — much more so than animals. In fog, a pilot never knows which way he is flying unless he keeps his eyes on his instruments. Otherwise he does not know whether the airplane is flying straight or banking, or diving, or climbing. But a dog standing beside him knows — you can see it standing at an angle, meeting the force of gravity. A human being does not have that sensibility. A blind person can not normally walk across a balancing beam, but in this respect a blind cat is barely distinguishable from a sighted cat. Both can walk along the narrowest ledges. They do this by means of entirely different, physical organs. But man clearly also has a balance-keeping organ, in the eye. We have four muscles for moving our eyes, plus two additional, so-called pulley muscles, above and below, which are directly connected to the sense organ of balance. We use this to see whether things are level or not. This is our way of determining our standpoint, about which I spoke before in relation to the organ of balance, which is directly connected to the eye. Just as the capacity of balance also works through the eye, so does the temperature sense, about which I shall speak presently. We speak of warm and cold colours. We also speak of sweet colours and dirty colours. We are talking, in this case, about the sense of taste. The sense of movement, too, is clearly connected with the eye — no sense is so mobile as the eye. When you see a triangle, you are walking it with your eyes. You are always walking with your eyes. At the same time you sense with your life sense whether what you see is pleasant or not. And when we meet each other in a personal way, which has to do with the ego sense, our eyes have a large role to play.

There obviously is only one concept that fits the eye — a concept we can accompany with a gesture — and that is that we can say that the eye is the *all-encompassing* sense.

Which star constellation belongs to the eye? It can be none other than the Virgin (*Virgo*, ♍), the largest constellation in the zodiac. The Virgin ensures that we immediately encounter the inner quality of things. And with this, one has actually expressed the secret of everything that has to do with the eye. What I expressed much more crudely at first, with the image of the exhibition, I can now indicate with the sign of the Virgin. For when nature, or the cosmos, reveals its inner quality on earth, it does so from the feminine point of view. This indicates the fascinating comprehensiveness of this sense; the Virgin is the world soul.

And so we pass on to the *warmth* or *temperature sense*. This is a different realm altogether. I want to start with an exercise. For this exercise I want you to fill a bowl with ice-cold water, and another bowl with fairly hot water. And in between you place a bowl with lukewarm water. Now put your left hand in the cold water and your right hand in the warm water, and keep them there for some time – at least two minutes. Then put both hands in the bowl with lukewarm water. It will give you a very funny feeling. If you have never done it, I urge you to do it a few times in order to let this experience sink in. For what happens? Your left hand, coming out of the cold water, finds the lukewarm water to be hot, while your right hand, coming out of the hot water, finds the lukewarm water to be cold. This is something the scientist finds intolerable, and therefore he prefers to use a thermometer. The funny thing is, though, that the thermometer does exactly the same thing as the human being. When I place a thermometer in cold water, the mercury rises to, say, 4 degrees, while a thermometer placed in the hot water will indicate 50 degrees or so. What happens when I place both thermometers in the bowl with lukewarm water? The thermometer out of the cold bath rises, and that out of the hot bath goes down, until eventually they both give the same reading. The first thermometer reacts as if to say: 'The lukewarm water isn't *that* cold', and the second reacts as if to say: 'The lukewarm water isn't *that* hot'. And this is what happens with our hands. We have to be patient for a moment, until we feel that they are at the same temperature.

What is it I wish to indicate here? I have tried to make it clear to you that we can experience temperature only when there is a *flow*. When something outside us is at the same temperature as we are, we do not experience 'hot' or 'cold'. Something has to happen between us and the world in order for us to experience temperature. There has to be flow. When, for instance, in the winter I grasp an outside door knob, heat flows from me to this door knob. I transmit heat. And as long as I transmit heat, I experience this door knob as cold. We can warm something up in our hands until it is as warm. At that point we sense the thing only with our sense of touch — not with our temperature sense. We no longer feel the temperature. Vice-versa, we can grasp a hot object, and heat flows to us from that object. This is simply a process of physics. Except that you are attending this lecture course because you wonder how it is that you can experience this. What forces do you use to experience this? And what is this feeling, this inner experience, when you perceive something as cold or hot, when you become aware of something cold or hot? I would like to express it this way: Cold makes us contract, while with heat we want to have as much room as possible. Cold has a chilling effect, while warmth evokes the opposite state of soul; warmth has an enthusing, stimulating effect. Warmth contains a stimulus. Why is this? What is behind this? What kind of peculiar mystery is this?

I have already said that in seeing colours the inner soul emerges — the soul turns itself inside-out. But there is something still more elementary, more simple than this. For what is required first of all to make an observation — be it of colour, of sound, of taste, or of odour? What is the first condition for having a sense impression? It is to open and close. And when you have opened something, when you have opened your eyes, for instance, do you see anything? Do you observe anything? No, first you need *attention*. Do you remember when I said to you in the first lecture that it is actually quite silly to deal with the senses one after another, because they all work together? Up till now I have not really dealt with anything but the warmth

sense in all of the senses. We have to *want* to observe
something, to *want* to hear something.

Picture yourself sitting at the window, dozing. You are not
watching, you are paying no attention, until all of a sudden you
see a cow running down the road with its tail up in the air. This
is something you have to see! Suddenly you are all attention.
For that is what is needed to be able to observe: *interest*. This is
the secret of the temperature sense.

So what do we do with the temperature sense? We do only
one thing in our soul: We want to meet the world. We are
interested in the world. Now, the world can respond to us in
either one of two ways. When we are interested, when we open
ourselves, we either get something back or we get nothing back.
When we get nothing back we experience cold, but when we do
receive something we experience a sense of warmth. This is the
secret of experiencing warmth, namely that our attention, our
interest, our absorption, is answered. We feel included. Do we
not need warmth from our fellow human beings? Can we leave
someone out in the cold? We always radiate interest, and expect
to be met with warmth.

Rudolf Steiner called this the first sense of man, although
initially it was located elsewhere, namely on the top of the head.
You have all heard of the 'third eye'. This third eye, however, is
not an eye. You still find it in reptiles, such as lizards. It is
located above the brain, below an opening in the skull (fontanelle). It looks much like a primitive eye. It turns out that some
lower animals can observe infrared with this organ. Infrared is
warmth. It is a warmth organ, therefore. In man it used to be an
organ with which he sought out the most comfortable places to
live. In the course of evolution this third eye has regressed to
become a small gland, the epiphysis, or pineal gland. Originally,
the pineal gland was located at the top of the head in humans,
too. In the embryonic stage you can still see this. Later the large
brain grows over the top of it. But at first the pineal gland is still
located high up, under the fontanelle — the opening in the still
transparent skull of the embryo.

Science does not really know what to make of the temperature sense. It is not understood how this sense functions, nor where it is located. It used to be thought that we have hot spots and cold spots everywhere. But the researchers all contradict each other. One day they report there are so and so many of these spots, but the next day, after subsequent experiments, it turns out there are many more. There are many different theories on this subject. I believe one theory to be the correct one, and this theory I have heard only once in my life. It is the following: Underneath the skin we have several very fine layers of capillary blood vessels. Also located underneath the skin are a large number of unexplained nerve endings. These are ordinary nerves, without any specialised apparatus at the nerve endings. These are the nerves I believe to be the temperature nerves — nerves that simply detect that warmth from the skin is withdrawn by the capillary blood vessels, or that it is given up. These are the least complicated nerves, for the least complicated process in the human soul takes place here. The human soul wishes to show an interest, and waits for something to show up. It does not have any specific instrument for doing this, but utilizes the 'interest nerves'. Is something approaching? Yes. This is the essence of warmth: Yes, we are involved, we are accepted by the universe, we can join in, we are stimulated, made enthusiastic. And we can express exactly the same thing in reverse, psychologically: We do not leave someone out in the cold; we are getting warm for something. This is what we probe for in nature with our interest. It is the archetypal sense, which has a primary presence in all other senses. The very essence, in fact, of every nerve is that it radiates interest, to see what comes back.

In anthroposophy we call this 'interest body' the *astral body*. The astral body is pure interest. It is typical of the animal – and the human kingdom. It represents being interested, curious, wanting to investigate everything in this world. This is what a nerve expresses, when it is undifferentiated, without further apparatus. It is probably difficult to visualize that this was at first a separate organ — the third eye, which subsequently disappeared, or, at least, regressed. But even though there is almost nothing left, something of importance still remains, withdrawn under the large brain. Because of the withdrawal of this organ, its capacity reappears in all nerves. It has sacrificed itself. And thus all senses, according to Rudolf Steiner, have been created from the warmth sense. It is an archetypal sense, which sacrifices itself in order to enable all other senses to be created from it as differentiations. You can see how marvellous a process this is — that something disappears, and twelve new versions reappear, as it were, including the original sense itself.

If you study anthroposophy further, you will find that in the work of Rudolf Steiner reference is made to the importance of the pineal gland, which natural science does not know what to make of; everything we absorb with our twelve senses comes together again in the pineal gland. Everything is gathered up here. I will not go into this further now — it would take me too deeply into the anthroposophical literature. Just take my word for it, for now.

Which sign of the zodiac is related to the temperature sense? You can probably guess. It is closely related to the Lion (*Leo*, ♌). This is the being, the animal being, that consists solely of enthusiasm, of interest. You can never become really human without having carefully observed lions and cats. If you could give yourself over to their movements, if you could move as gracefully as a cat does when it curves its tail around itself, you would realize how warm, vital, eurhythmic this is. Nowhere is there any rigidity in these animals. Just try to move your nail! You can not do it. But lions and cats have such vitality that they can move even their claws. This radiant warmth, this glow of interest, is present right down to the polarity of dead matter. No other animal can as genuinely enjoy its environment, lie down in lazy comfort, purring, or be as expressive in its gentleness, or in its cruelty, its growls, it terrifying roar, its silent, gliding stalk, its sudden leap, its graceful stretching, sitting, climbing. Everything from claws to the tip of the tail is under control. This is also the image of the Lion in the cosmos.

This is all I wanted to say about the warmth sense, the temperature sense.

Chapter Five

Hearing

Just as on previous occasions, I will start by recapitulating the senses I have dealt with so far. We started off this lecture cycle with the four senses typically associated with the body: touch, the life sense, the sense of self-movement, and balance; touch makes us aware of our bodily nature; the life sense brings to consciousness the fact that we are full of life processes, that we have a constitution, that we are ill or healthy; the sense of self-movement brings to our attention the degree of control we have over our physical body, the dynamic capability with which we express ourselves through our body, with which we can move; and about balance, finally, I told you that the entire human being is constituted as a being of balance. Just as with touch we leave the world, so by means of balance we re-enter the world. We can only maintain our balance with reference to the world.

After these four body-related senses, we spoke extensively about the four well-known soul senses — those of smell, taste, vision, and temperature. With these four senses you will find a kind of repetition of the way the body-related senses function. In smell we are really dealing with something dry (when you have a cold you can not smell anything), something shadowy, something that has died, as it were. The scent of a plant, however alive the plant, is after all only an emanation, a material secretion. We have seen how smell affects us in an aggressive way, to which, in turn, we react quite aggressively. Odour affects our instinctive nature, and we react to it instinctively. You could say it has something of a will-related character.

With respect to taste — this curious threshold function in the human being — I explained that it is, in fact, the most degenerate sense in man because, more and more, we taste only whether something is pleasing to the palate or not, whereas once upon a time our taste was, as it must become again, the means of ascertaining whether or not something is good for our constitution — whether it is wholesome or not, just as we do with our life sense, except that with taste it is to a greater degree a matter of our own choice whether we will develop this capability or not.

If we had only these two body-related senses, that is, only smell and taste, we would, of course, be quite dreamy, as if living in a trance. Only through the eye is the world opened to us. The eye is an incredible organ, which captures everything in one glance. This allows us to see the world as a whole. The concept of beauty, for instance, could never arise in the human being if he had no eyes. I explained to you how colour reveals the inner nature of the world. Through colour, the soul of the world is made visible. By means of colour we meet the world soul. And just as we ourselves are beings that live between light and dark — just as we turn outward to the light and inward to darkness, within ourselves — so colour displays itself between these same two polarities. Everyone who thinks of yellow immediately senses that it has to do with light, while blue and black are representative of darkness. Goethe taught us much on this subject. We also encounter the relation between colour and soul moods in the wisdom of language. We speak of joyous colours and sombre colours, for example. This is impossible with taste. Who would ever say something like: 'These carrots taste joyous', or speak of 'sombre onions'? No, we are dealing with a realm here in which the soul shows itself directly, in which our soul is exposed. We do not reveal soul moods only as a result of life experiences; colour affects the soul itself. Whatever reveals itself to us is experienced directly as joyous or sad.

In anthroposophy, this is called the *sentient soul*. An even better designation would be *mood soul*, because it has to do with soul moods. Are you not always in a particular mood in relation to different things? And is this not especially true when you are seeing? This is where we are really concerned with the mood soul, with what we do in our soul relative to the world soul.

Just as smell has a willful character, and taste, because of its more intimate nature, is more emotional, so does vision have a sort of thought process associated with it, which becomes active as soon as you open your eyes. We always think 'through' the eyes. We would not be thinking beings if we did not have eyes. I spoke about optical illusions in this context. These are possible only because there is thinking playing into vision. Please, do not draw the conclusion that the blind can not think. We are talking about the general principle of the senses, namely that certain senses — such as, in this instance, vision — have been given to mankind with a purpose. We could not be thinking beings if mankind had not been given the capacity for vision.

Just try and take note of what you think about. Is this not related largely to visual impressions? I demonstrated to you that even when we talk about smell or taste, we 'see' our nose or our mouth in front of us. We find it extremely difficult to eliminate our eyes, simply because we are thinking beings. All of science is in a way a world of vision. We can use an = sign for knowledge = insight!

And finally we encountered the temperature sense — eighth in this series. Even though I dealt with this sense as number eight, the temperature sense is really the first sense given to man. For it is owing to the temperature sense that we are able to meet the world. This is something that man has in common with the animal. Plants are not able to observe anything. Only the animal and the human being can observe, and that is because they want to meet the world out of their own volition. This is called the astral body. In the astral body (the soul body) we are dealing with the temperature sense. An animal, however, is motivated only by its basic drives, and is not, therefore, conscious of the fact that it can observe, that it is meeting the world. Man, on the other hand, does have consciousness, and as a result has a conscious awareness of participation in the world. And participation in the world is expressed in the temperature sense. We can say that warmth expresses involvement, joining in (when

our interest, apparently, has found response), and cold expresses
exclusion (we are left out in the cold). With this we have
expressed the most elementary, archetypal aspect of the human
soul. Man always wants to connect with the world around him
by radiating warmth and receiving warmth.

Many of you may think that *hearing* also belongs in the
category of the soul senses. I hope I can make plain to you in the
following that with respect to hearing we enter into a fundamentally different world.

I would like to start with the question: How does sound come
about? Try to imagine that you have never in your life heard any
sound. You have seen everything − even a beautiful brass bell
− but you do not know that sound exists, and that this brass bell
serves a purpose other than its ornamental one. And then, when
you are already an adult, you happen to strike this bell for the
first time. And for the first time you hear its sound. What would
happen to you? You would probably be pretty shaken. And you
would wonder just how is it possible that this thing you have
always seen as merely a beautifully shiny object turns out to be a
beautifully sounding object as well. Would you believe it if you
were told that these are just a few 'vibrations', which can be
precisely calculated and represented in a graph? I am sure this
would be meaningless to you, for what would this have to do
with the essence of the sound you were hearing?

What is required to let something resound? When you strike
a lump of wet clay, it does not resound. No, it has to be
something hard, earthly, in order for it to resound when we tap
it. But this is not the only condition for making sound. If you hit
a piece of ore that is still in the ground, it does not make much of
a sound either, does it! As long as something is stuck fast in the
earth, it does not resound. What we need in order to produce
real resonance is something quite hard, very earthly, which is
no longer buried in the earth. Only the earthly that has been
separated from the earth resounds. We have to lift it, release it,
from its earth-bound state. Metals are the best example. Only
when the metal has been specially hardened in the smelter and

the earthly impurities have been removed, and we then allow it to float in the air, can beautiful tones be produced. Just suppose that it were possible to let the hardened, purified metal float in the air, without it being held anywhere. We could then produce the most beautiful resonance by striking it. And, indeed, by striking it, a vibration, a movement is generated.

There is a remarkable thing about this vibrating movement. You all know that the earth revolves. This was confirmed by means of the large pendulum in the Pantheon in Paris. The movement of this pendulum is not constant. Its velocity changes continuously. From the highest point downwards it first accelerates, and then decelerates, until it stops momentarily upon reaching the highest point again, then accelerating and decelerating on its return swing. The movement, therefore, is itself in movement.

In addition, this moving movement orientates itself to the universe. The vertical plane in which the pendulum swings is constant with respect to the universe. However, because the earth revolves in the universe, it appears as if the direction of the pendulum changes. But it is the position of the earth that changes.

This is how it is with the movements, the vibrations, of sound. These are moving movements (just like that of the pendulum, which is similarly 'loosened from the earth'), which orientate themselves to the universe.

When you hold this image of something earthly that has been made unearthly and emits a super-movement, a vibration oriented to the universe, you begin to understand something about sound. Matter is brought into a condition that is the opposite of its natural state. This is what I wanted to demonstrate to you. This is the only way you can really begin to comprehend something about the miracle of sound, namely that sound is only created when we release from the earth something hard, something very earthly, which of itself can never move, and then bring it into a super-movement that is no longer earth-orientated.

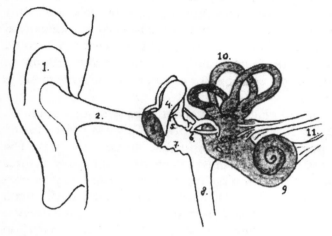

Outer ear	7. Tympanic cavity
1. Concha	8. Eustachian tube
2. Auditory canal	
3. Eardrum	*Inner ear*
Middle ear	9. Cochlea
4. Hammer	10. Three semi-circular
5. Anvil	canals
6. Stirrup	11. Nerves

Section of the organ of hearing

Now that we know what the nature of sound is, we come to the question: How does the instrument that senses sound — the ear — work?

The ear consists of three parts: the outer ear, the middle ear, and the inner ear. The outer ear consists of the concha (shell of the ear), the auditory canal, and the eardrum. In the middle ear there are three small bones: hammer, anvil, and stirrup. A tube leads from the middle ear to the mouth, called the Eustachian tube, which becomes plugged when you have a cold. The inner ear, finally, consists of the so-called cochlea, which is connected to the three semi-circular canals — the organ of balance we discussed earlier.

The organ of hearing starts its development on the surface, as

most of the other sense organs do. First there is a small
indentation in the skin, in the area of the so-called gill slit,
from which the breathing and the eating apparatus are developed
as well. This occurs in an early phase of embryonic development,
when the eyes are only in the beginning stage at the sides of the
head. Gradually, however, the eyes move forward, while the
location of the hearing organs moves back. The ears end up in a
different location, therefore, from the one where they started.
Meanwhile, the indentation in the skin becomes a fluid-filled
vesicle, out of which, in a subsequent stage, the three semi-
circular canals of the organ of balance are formed. So, our inner
ear gradually takes shape from a small area of skin on the
surface. At the same time as the vesicles are formed they move
to a greater depth under the skin, and are transformed into the
cochlea and the three semi-circular canals. What was at first
skin ends up deep down in the petrous bone in the base of the
skull. This is only the case in man. When you look at an animal
skull, including that of a mammal, you can see that nothing like

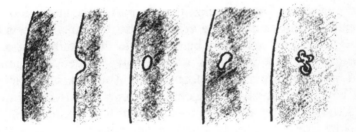

Diagrammatic representation of the development of the inner ear

the same depth is attained. The inner ear hangs somewhere
under the petrous bone. Only in man is it tucked away safely
deep down in the hardest bone of the entire body.

Now that we have seen how the inner ear develops from
something on the surface moving deep down inside, I will
continue with the ear-bones in the middle ear. These ear-
bones are created because, among others, a section of the jaw

draws back and subsequently is transformed into the ear-bones, together with what will later become the tongue-bone. Perhaps you can visualize this most easily with the help of the following example: Just as an airplane, on take-off, draws up its under-carriage, so a part of the jaw draws back to metamorphose into the ear-bones.

The outer ear, finally, develops out of a few skin tubercles, which grow to form the external ear shell.

The ear also has a peculiar development, therefore. Whereas in the case of the eyes it was the brain that moved forward and 'blossomed' on the surface, hearing comes about as a result of something that was on the outside at first, and moves inward, becomes internal, where, in conjunction with the jaw, it forms the organ of hearing.

At the university where I went to medical school, one of the professors used to say, in reference to the descent of the higher animals, in which he included man: 'At the moment, we hear with the part we used to eat with'. He meant it as a joke, but it is true enough, and there is no greater contrast than that between eating and hearing. This moreover, contains the secret of 'internalizing'. Do you realize that the part of the body used for breathing and eating is the very last that remains functional? The last things a human being can do are swallowing and breathing. These functions are carefully guarded, for eating and breathing are man's sources of life. And this is the part of the body from which hearing develops; from here it withdraws, and subsequently assumes an entirely different function.

Now I have to explain a new movement to you — one that may be an entirely new concept to you. I can walk faster and faster, or I can walk more and more slowly, until at a given moment I stand still. Can you imagine a movement, however, that is even more 'still' than standing still? So, something (for example, the jaw) moves rapidly at first, and then more slowly, until it stops all movement and remains at rest. When you extrapolate this sequence past the state in which the object is at rest, you can perhaps visualize how we come to a point where it is 'being moved'. In other words: Stiller than still is to *be* moved, just as owning less than nothing means being in debt (negative ownership, therefore). Our ear-bones, in fact, are *being* moved. From the most instinctive part of the body, where by breathing and eating we fight for survival, and in which the strongest of all muscles are located, something withdraws, which becomes so still, which turns so much inward when it seeks seclusion in our hardest bone, which becomes so restful, that it allows itself to *be* moved. For the purpose of even the few small muscles attached to our ear-bones is to attenuate the induced motion should it become too strong.

Now I will continue with the outer ear. I have already said that this is no more than a few tubercles that develop into the external ear. The odd thing is, the human ear (and that of the monkeys and man-apes as well) is curled inward instead of being placed on the head like a pair of funnel-like protuberances, as is the case with, for example, the horse. Why is this? Would a funnel not be more practical? When someone articulates poorly, or the sound is soft, we have to make a funnel with our hand in order to hear better. I suggest to you, however, that although you might hear better, you could never listen if your ears were constructed like funnels. If you pay attention, you will notice that a horse does not listen, but 'looks' with his ears; because he can not listen, he can still move his ears. This capacity is held back in man. Even though there are plenty of muscles in the external ear, man can not move his ears, and certainly not point them forward.

And now we can begin to understand something of the human spirit. The human spirit is higher than the human soul. The soul has to do with reacting to the world and 'doing' in the world. Through the spirit we can do something *about ourselves*. The striking thing about hearing is that it derives from the sphere where the human being strives to do everything through his own activity, but has withdrawn from such activity. Because of the process of overcoming the instinctive it is possible for man to internalize. For internalizing is a process. For this reason the ear has to be started externally and go through an internalizing process. If the ear were initiated internally, there would be no internalizing. The human being has to go through this development. The great thing about embryology as a science is that it allows us to see how the different organs develop. Just as the eye develops on the basis of curiosity and meets the superficial world displayed before it only because of this curiosity, so the development of the ear takes its course starting from the external, and going deeper and deeper into the internal.

Now I still have to say something further about this inner nature. You know that bone always has bone marrow. Bone marrow is man's source of life, from the metabolic point of view; it is what keeps the blood alive. Now, in the petrous bone, into which hearing has withdrawn, something odd happens. At a certain moment we see in embryology how hosts of cells go to this petrous bone to 'eat' the bone marrow — our source of life. The most 'holy space' is devoured and becomes a dead, cave-like space. We can recognize the same process in this. For this bone is at first quite alive, but then all this life is removed. Cavities are created. Obvious, you will say, for there have to be resonant cavities. True, but what I find so interesting is that these cavities might just as well have been created in the first place, without this process of removal of life being of any importance. But no, by careful study of embryology we find the meaning behind all this.

Thus, embryology teaches us that our organ of hearing matches its purpose exactly, namely to help us free ourselves from the instinctive. For what is an instinct? It is something that binds us to the earth. So, just as a metal has to be removed from the earth, has to be released from its earth-bound state in order to produce sound, so does the organ that has to receive the sound have to be liberated from the earth, from the instinctive. And so you can understand that with our hearing we penetrate much more deeply into reality than we do with our eyes, which, after all, only perceive the surface of things. Our temperature sense already goes a little deeper. I can still fool your eyes, but with the temperature sense this is already harder to do. With the temperature sense we are dealing not merely with the outside of things, but we feel what something is like more or less through and through. But temperature is still dependent on the environment. In the cold we observe an object to be in a different condition from what it is in a warm environment. But when we hear something, we really hear what that something *is*. By tapping a wine glass, we can hear whether it is crystal. Italian bus drivers have a small marble plate beside their cash register, on which they drop coins to ascertain whether they are real. In sound, the true voice of things, the deepest inner nature, is made manifest. Silver has a particular sound; other metals sound different. Crystal has a clear sound while glass sounds quite different. With our hearing we penetrate deeply into the inner nature of matter because we become stiller than still, and renounce all earthly desire.

And yet, nowhere else in the human being do we find anything as mechanical taking place as the vibrations of sound. Nowhere else is the outer world admitted as deeply. Nowhere else is there a drumming like that of the ear-bones. But we hear no drumming. We hear a sound! Is that not a great mystery? A purely mechanical process works in us. We can measure everything related to sound with great precision. We can record it. We can put numbers to it. It is as earthly as could be. Nowhere does the earthly penetrate to the extent it does here, but we hear something totally unearthly. This is the incomprehensible thing about it. We do not hear 87 or 493 vibrations. We hear a tone.

Here I have to introduce yet another term in order to clarify something else we are dealing with in the internalizing process, namely the term *erase*. What is this internalizing, really? It is an erasing phenomenon. I will clarify this with the following example. What happens when you read? Do you read each letter separately? No, if you did you would be spelling, the way young children do when they are just learning to read. You have to erase the individual characters, these specially shaped black ink marks on the paper, in order to be able to read the whole. Reading, incidentally, is something in which the ear plays a large role. You actually 'hear' the word, even when you read silently. In earlier times, people always had to read aloud in the same way beginners do today.

Just as the process from spelling to reading is an erasing process, so we can say with respect to hearing that we erase the sound vibrations. We never hear a vibration, in fact, we eliminate it. We erase everything earthly, and this is possible because the organ of hearing has freed itself from its instinctive aspect; the ear has been internalized.

If you learn to look at it this way, you begin to comprehend much about hearing. You will now also realize that one can erase not only the acoustic vibrations (one always does this automatically anyway), but that one can erase the individual tones. One can play a C and a G to make a fourth. One can play two notes on the piano. What happens? One erases them and only hears the interval. When one hears an interval, one no longer hears the first tone and the one after it separately. One also hears a melody this way. A melody is never a sequence of tones. If one heard a number of tones, one would no longer hear a melody. The melody is something that arises from between the tones. And in order to be able to hear this, one has to erase the separate tones.

Are you beginning to see that we are not dealing here with a soul quality? We have truly entered the spiritual realm. This is why music is so closely related to mathematics. In music, too, we can express everything in numbers. With colour you can not do this. Colour can not be defined by mathematical formulae, but sound can be. You can count how many acoustic vibrations there are in an interval. You can express the relationship in the interval precisely, in numbers. For mathematics is, in fact, inward hearing. It is spirit.

Which star constellation is related to what we have been talking about in regard to hearing? It will probably be more or less obvious to you why hearing is related to the Crab (*Cancer*, ♋) when I give you the symbolic representation of the sign for this sense: . For this symbol implies that where one world ceases, another world begins. Which are the two worlds of Cancer? In order to explain this, I shall first have to speak about a few general concepts that have to do with the *spiral* form.

When we look at the universe, we see giant spiral nebulae

with thousands of stars. Where does it all come from? Where do these visible stars come from? Now, the archetypal law of the visible is that the visible is always created from the invisible. Everything that has been created has come into being out of the invisible. Therefore our visible stars and nebulae have also arisen from the invisible. It is only the visible half that we observe, which has parted from the invisible. *Every creation, in fact, is that which has been released from the ultimate source, such that the creative element is transformed into the creation.* This is the shortest possible formulation of the origin of the universe.

The Crab has power over matter in a peculiar way. It sheds its skin several times during its period of growth. It dissolves the hard substances of its armour, and sublimates these as small stones in its stomach. Later, these stones are dissolved again and transported to the new skin for the construction of a new shell.

The process in the macrocosm I have just described also occurs in the microcosm, namely in our belly, in our intestine. Our intestinal system is also a spiral. In embryology you can see that our intestine gets started as a simple tube, which at a given moment begins to form turns, so that we end up with a spiral. Now, everybody knows that our having a long intestine is useful. But why does it have to be a spiral? What does this express? What does this signify? What happens in the intestine? I already discussed this in connection with taste. We eat the macrocosm, we eat something from the world, which has to disappear completely. It has to be entirely absorbed. It has to lose its original structure because no outside matter or anything akin to it, none of its properties, are supposed to enter the human being directly. It has to be totally destroyed. The macrocosm is reduced to zero, as it were, in order to be subsequently assimilated; it is adapted to the internal substance. Everything foreign in it has to be removed. The macrocosm, therefore, becomes our own substance, and this is possible only by way of a spiral. The intestinal spiral expresses the end of the outside world, and the creation by the human being of a world of his own.

Now you will also understand why the cochlea in the ear is

constructed as a spiral. It can not be a zigzag, a line, or a circle.
It has to be a spiral, for this is an expression of the fact that here
the dead, mechanical world ceases, and that the spiritual element is liberated from matter. We recognize this movement of
the cessation of one condition and the consequent creation of a
new, opposite condition in the sign of Cancer. In the zodiac this
sign is positioned opposite that of Capricorn, the sign of
balance.

You can see how we have to make enormous detours in order
to make some simple facts comprehensible. It is a mystery to
the natural scientist why the organ of balance and the cochlea
have the same origin. From the natural scientific point of view
alone you can never explain what balance has to do with
hearing. Only by looking clearly at the development of the
human being, in which embryology is of help because the
microcosmic creation of the individual is a mirror image of the
macrocosmic creation of humanity as a whole, can we gain some
insight into the fact that our hearing and our balance have been
created from the same tubercle. It is because they are polar
opposites. With our organ of balance we connect with the earth
– we orient ourselves in earthly space. Only when we have an
earthly orientation can we be elevated from this earthly space.
And how are we elevated? How can we once again enter the
spirit realm, the cosmos? By listening! With our hearing! We
have to eliminate our external balance in order to gain inner
balance. We can regard listening to music as 'taking a walk'
using our inner balance – the balance between high and low,
and slow and fast. If this balance is not present in a piece of
music, we rightfully speak of an imbalance in the music.

Now, we can all experience that the more we recline in a
chair, the more we lie back, and the less we maintain our
balance and therefore feel our body, the better can we hear the
beauty of music. Somebody who nods his head keeping time
with the music is not really hearing any better. On the contrary.
We actually have to do less than nothing. We can hear well only
when we eliminate our earth organ, our organ of balance. But
we must have such an organ to begin with.

In the next part of this lecture, Dr. Soesman demonstrated several different musical instruments. Obviously it is not possible to give the reader the same experience as the audience in the lecture hall. However, an attempt has been made in the following to give the reader a clear idea of what the speaker tried to convey to his listeners.

What is the very essence of music? Music consists of only three things: the right pitch, the right tone length, and the right volume. That is all. These are three inner dimensions; just as we have three outer dimensions in balance: height, width and depth.

I will demonstrate by means of a number of examples how strongly our body is affected by music. You are all familiar with the sound of somebody scratching his nail across a blackboard. It sounds awful. It is unbearable. You 'hear' this with your skin. You feel how it grates on your skin. You do not hear this with your ears at all. In an extreme example like this, you become aware of several things: You notice that this kind of sound does not go inside you, but remains at the surface. If, on the other hand, you listen to a beautiful piece on the violin, you experience this somewhere else. The sound of the violin, if it is pure, is really related to the feelings. It does not remain on the surface of the skin, but it penetrates under the skin as if it were caressing you there. This is how it speaks to the feelings. And it is no coincidence that a violin played offkey, with a scratching sound, is so similar to scratching a blackboard. The effects on our body are close together.

Another exercise we can do with the violin is to try to experience what happens to the sound in our body when we hear a scale played from low to high. We notice, specially when we are standing, that the tones climb up in our body like a growing vine.

Just as we feel the sound of the violin underneath our skin, there are other instruments we can feel elsewhere. If, for instance, a wood xylophone is played, and we really try to concentrate on the effect the sound has on our body, we become aware that this sound goes deeper than that of the violin. It penetrates almost to the skeleton. This is not the case with a metal xylophone, which is fundamentally different from

a wood xylophone. The sound of striking wood affects our
bones much more than the sound of striking metal. The latter
we 'hear' more in our muscle, like a massage. While wood gives
us the impression of having touched bottom in ourselves, in our
bones, we experience the sound of metal in the blood coursing
through our muscles.

The sound of the flute also works in us at a deeper level. And
yet it is quite different again from wood and metal percussion
instruments. A flute specifically affects our breathing organism.
Just as the violin strokes our skin, so the flute affects our
breathing system.

Another wind instrument, the horn, or trumpet, is for many
people more difficult to relate to. These instruments also affect
the breathing system, but they go much deeper, into the part
where the air is processed in the body — in the blood, in the
heart, and perhaps the image of a trumpeting angel illustrates
this. In playing the trumpet, the heart of the angel speaks.

And which part of the body would be affected by the harp
and the lyre? Is there any instrument that sounds as tenderly
and feelingly as the harp or lyre? Is there any other instrument
as soothing, as restoring, in fact? The sounds of the harp and
lyre are indeed perceived by the nerves. If ever there should be a
requirement for a music therapy for nervous disorders, it would
have to be a therapy based on the lyre. This is how beneficial,
how healing the sound of the lyre can be.

The intent of these exercises is not that you should learn to
listen consciously with different parts of your body. We should,
in fact, forget all about this when we really want to listen. As an
exercise, however, it is interesting because, as I have tried to
demonstrate to you with these musical instruments, sound is
actually grasped first in a physical way, after which (and, once
again, this fortunately takes place subconsciously most of the
time) we erase it in order to 'take a leap' into the spiritual world.
With hearing, therefore, the *social element* is brought into our
culture. It raises us above ourselves because it first affects us
physically. It really overcomes the physical, erases it.

What forces do we use for this? When we go down the list of senses, it seems nothing is left. We have seen how immensely great powers are available to us in connection with the 'lower' senses — touch, life sense, selfmovement sense, and balance. We have also seen that all soul forces have been assigned to the four soul senses — the consciousness soul and will in connection with smell, the intellectual/mind soul and feeling with taste, the sentient soul and thinking with sight, and our interest, our attention, with the temperature sense. What is available to us for hearing? There is nothing left!

Rudolf Steiner states that the human being himself can not hear, that other beings have to help. We can hear because we get help from the souls of the angels. We hear through the souls of the angels instead of through our own soul. This is because — and this may sound unkind — we are too egotistical. The truly social, unselfish, loving element is not yet present in man. It will take quite some time for this to be developed. Of course, we often try to be social and to act in a loving way. But angelic beings do this as a matter of course. They always act in a wholly unselfish way as protectors of man. This is why it is the angels that work in us in this truly social, truly spiritual sense — that of hearing.

Rudolf Steiner made a very curious remark about our organ of hearing, to the effect that although the temperature sense was the first sense of man, hearing was there even before the beginning. We are dealing here with an 'impossible' sense, therefore, one that existed before creation. I explained to you that all that is created is, in a way, separated out, released from the cosmos as a materialization. Therefore we have in hearing the great paradox of a sense that is entirely earthly, and functions in a thoroughly earthly way, and yet is constructed directly out of heavenly substance, with the angels — beings of the heavenly hierarchies, ranked directly above man — working into it. Sound is a reality. It is not a semblance, not an image, as with sight, but reality itself. You will never dance in front of a painting, but it is hard to keep still with music. Music touches us in our muscle and bones. It is a dynamic power, and because of its heavenly origin it can also become the most demonic power. Demons know exactly where to take hold of the human being, and that is why they do it through music. There is nothing as demonic as music can be, for it embodies the highest powers, and it is difficult for the human being to become conscious of these powers and to resist them when they are demonic.

Thus we find in hearing the essence of the social element: something that has been held back, has not become earthly, but has remained heavenly, which is present in man in an elementary way in the act of hearing. Hearing always means giving ourselves up and giving ourselves over to something, or someone, else. We are as yet quite incapable of doing this with our own forces. In every communion that comes about with each relationship between two people, help and protection is always needed from guardian angels.

Finally, I would like to bring the following to your attention. We live at a time in which everything has to be recorded, for all eternity. Everything has to be stored in a "memory", has to be "mummified": photographs, films, cassettes, etc. Our materalism throws everything into one big heap, everything is permissible: there is no distinction between image and sound.

By means of spiritual science, however, we can find out that there is a great difference between what we make pictures of, and what we record as sound. A picture is always semblance. Sound is real. Nothing in the way of pictures has any influence on the dead. It is different in the case of sound, and in particular in the case of the human voice. When we record, we forcibly hold on to something that is past. Music and speech have to be forever recreated in time. When we realize this inwardly, we can also understand that this is not a matter of indifference when we mechanically "turn on" the preserved, magnetically "canned" voice of someone at will. This retards the development of those souls that have returned to the spirit world to continue there. To bring something to life in one's memory, using one's own energies, is very meaningful, on the other hand, as imperfect as it may be. To be joined with the spirit requires a deeper sense of responsibility.

Chapter Six

The speech sense, concept sense, and ego sense

This time we shall have to conclude. I told you on the first occasion we would talk about the first chapter of anthroposophy. Meanwhile you have discovered what you got yourselves into with that idea 'first chapter'. I did warn you that this first chapter is quite all-embracing. Now I can tell you that whatever chapter of anthroposophy you take, it is always all-embracing. This is what is new and special about anthroposophy. It is not based on reductionism. On the contrary, even if we deal with a small component, we can only understand it from the all-embracing totality. This totality is never comprehensible from the single detail. It is often assumed that we can understand everything from tiny atoms. This is not so. In order to understand a small atom, a small component, we need an all-embracing world view.

Last time we talked only about hearing. I tried to explain that in hearing we are dealing with a *social sense*, a *spiritual sense*. We spoke about how sound arises, and about hearing sound. We saw how our organ of hearing has developed from a small section of body surface and a small piece of jaw bone. I tried to explain what this means, in its essence. Now we know where in our body we 'hear' the sound of different musical instruments, and what is the best way to listen to music: by ignoring our body as much as possible. We now realize that although we know that there are sound vibrations, this is *not* what we hear. In fact, we disregard these vibrations in order to get to the tone itself, which reveals the innermost character of matter. Consequently, we can gain much more of an understanding of matter by listening to music than by looking through a microscope. Science, too, has discovered this, although from a quite different perspective. You know how the chemical elements are arranged in the so-called periodic table. It was discovered that all elements can be categorized according to a certain rhythm, a musical rhythm, a kind of scale, in which seven elements are placed in a certain order, and the eighth has properties similar to the first, etc. This is known as the periodic table of Mendelejev.

We also came to an understanding of why the organ of balance and the organ of hearing are located so closely together, why they are created from a common origin. And, finally, I conveyed to you how in the distant future we will be able, through hearing, to develop a social sense and to act truly socially, but that at present the angel beings have to assist us in this — that they, in fact, 'manage' our hearing.

Tonight I want to deal with the last three senses: the speech sense, the concept sense, and the ego sense. These three senses were actually discovered by Rudolf Steiner. Since then, others have also described them. For instance, there is a detailed study of the ego sense by Buitendijk in his treatise on 'the human phenomenon'. But Rudolf Steiner was the first to mention these three senses. And because they are new and unfamiliar, one has to make a special effort to explain what they really are. The terminology is still lacking. This is always the case with something new. Words do not work too well. One has to read between the lines in order to grasp what is meant.

When you hear that the speech or language sense means that we hear language, that we notice that someone speaks a language, you may think: 'It is quite obvious that we hear this, after all, we have an organ for hearing.' Rudolf Steiner, however, showed that it makes quite a difference whether we listen to music or hear a language spoken. It is fundamentally different. A language is not a complicated kind of music — it is not a kind of musical arrangement, as if, when we pronounce such and such a sequence of tones, we mean this or that. Rudolf Steiner pointed out that the language sense differs as much from hearing as, for example, the temperature sense from seeing, or smell from taste. To hear music, or tones, or the musical element, is in principle different from hearing a language. Just try and do the following. Turn on a radio that can receive many stations, and tune it to a station playing music you never heard before, which is completely unfamiliar to you. Then tune to a station on which you hear a language you do not know at all. Despite the fact that you do not know either the music or the language, you know right away one is music and the other a language. You hear it immediately. If this is what you hear, then what is the difference? This is a tough question. We are always good at explaining similarities. A cat and a dog are both animals with four legs. That is easy to explain. But what is the difference between a dog and a cat? We could talk about that for hours. It is the same with music and language.

What is it that happens in your soul when you hear music, and what happens when you hear a language? You notice that something happens, but can you describe and explain it? In the first place, it has nothing to do with the fact that a language may be difficult — you do not hear this at all. Music can also be pretty complicated, particularly if it is music from an altogether different culture, or modern music. And still, we can hear that it is music. What, then, is language?

Now, some people will probably say: 'Is a language not music, too? Do we not speak of the musical element of language?' This is true. We distinguish one language from another because the musical element is different. But this musical element is not in the foreground. Each language is musical to an extent, but it is still not music. There is a much deeper secret behind language. We can compose music. But to make a living language is impossible. It has been tried, with Esperanto, for instance, but the result is quite artificial. Despite the fact that the structure of Esperanto, according to its 'creators', is logical, simple, more practical than all living languages, it will never be a real language. It is a typical non-language. It is nothing but a lot of agreements. This is because language is not a complicated musical agreement, but something of an entirely different order. Someone who can make music is not necessarily a creative linguist. There are people who have a flair for languages, and others who have a musical talent. These two do not necessarily go together. One can not say that musically gifted people can easily learn to speak foreign languages. Musicians often have a feel for mathematics, strangely enough, but the flair for languages and the flair for music are different 'flairs'.

If I really want to hear a language, I must first suppress, disregard, the music in it. I should take no notice of the musical element. It is very interesting to try to do this, just as it was interesting to try to hear a musical instrument somewhere in your body. For if you want to become clear about what the musical element is in a language, and you want to compare this with the musical element in another language, you can only do that by taking special notice. And then you no longer hear *what* is said, but *how* it is said. With the ordinary way of listening, we do include the musical element, but it is not taken in consciously. We have to disregard it in order to meet a language in its pure form. *Language is language.*

One can not tinker with a language. Just try to introduce a new word into the vocabulary. It is very difficult and seldom successful. A new word just arises in the language. Suddenly it is 'in'. Often we do not even know where it came from.

It is well known that there have been certain language reformers. The German language is for an important part due to Luther, who had a special linguistic ability. Italian is largely attributable to Dante; he really formed it. Only few people, only highly gifted artists, are able to form a language. This is because the wisdom of language is of a different world, which can not be likened to the world of the musical element. Then what is this special world, which we enter when we have eliminated the musical element?

You know that language consists of vowels and consonants. You may say: 'Is this not the same as in music, do you not have similar elements there? I will show you that this is not the case. With the elements of language you can do something you can never do with tones on the piano. For example, A on the piano is absolutely fixed. It has a given number of vibrations. It is fixed, and because of this we have named it 'A'. The fifth takes us further up on the scale, and we call this 'E'. Music is fixed such that every tone has its place. But with the letter A, the vowel, I can do something quite remarkable. The pitch of the vowel A is not fixed. I can pronounce A with a low base voice, or I can say it in a high, squeaky voice. It remains A. I can even sing a melody with the vowel A. It never becomes E. I can maintain the A at every pitch. I can sing a vowel, and, with slightly more effort, a consonant as well. I can hum the N at different pitches. I can sing the elements of a language separately, therefore. I can not do this with the separate elements in music.

In what other way can we sing, or make, melodies? We can do this with a violin, or a flute, or a piano. In fact, we can make melodies on all musical instruments when we produce different tones. So, actually the values of the different vowels and consonants are comparable to the values of the different instruments. You can do the same thing with a vowel or a consonant that you can do with a violin. This is of a higher order than music. When you listen to language, to the word 'plant', for instance, you do not pay any attention to its musical quality. You may spell it: p−l−a−n−t, or you may say it in a low or a high voice. You may sing it, with musical tone formation. But something incomprehensible keeps taking place. You are continually disregarding the musical element, while in effect you are hearing a sequence of musical instruments one after the other. Imagine hearing a guitar, then a flute, next a violin, and subsequently a trumpet, all in quick succession. As music, it would sound terrible. And yet, this is what you hear in language. In language, all you hear is one instrument after another.

On one occasion I met someone who also described it like this. It was the English educator and author A.C. Harwood. During a trip he lay down on the bed in his hotel room, dead tired, trying to get to sleep. Just as he was about to fall asleep, people came into the room beside his. As a result, he could not get to sleep, and was forced, as it were, to listen to these other hotel guests talking, while in a tired, dreamy state. They spoke a language unfamiliar to him; he did not understand what was said. He heard their language in its pure form, as a phenomenon, and he was so tired that his intellect was inactive. What did Harwood experience? He expressed it much more aptly than I have ever been able to: 'It was like listening to an air, played on a number of successive instruments, though of course the transition was not abrupt, but organic.' (A.C. Harwood, *The Golden Blade*, 1953)

Now, when you hear this statement, you can see how in a dreamy condition someone experienced the very same thing I have tried to explain to you at length. What becomes apparent is that in hearing language we have the amazing ability, which goes beyond that of mere hearing, not only to disregard vibrations and separate tones in order to hear an interval, but even to disregard the entire musical element − all of the music. And when you appreciate this clearly, you can see that the vowels and consonants are no less than manifestations of a higher order, that they are cosmic instruments. We are able to tie a whole sequence of these instruments directly together. This, indeed, is of a much higher order than merely hearing tones, hearing a melody of tones. Here you have a melody of instruments, one after the other, forming a language.

This speech sense, or language sense, as Rudolf Steiner also called it, is the direct opposite of the self-movement sense. I have explained that the sense of self-movement is the ability to observe, to participate in, to experience, our own movements. Now, what are we actually doing when we participate in our own movements? There are two kinds of movement: adaptive movement and emotional, expressive movement. All movements adapted to an instrument are adaptive movements, such as when I do carpentry or drive a car. Even when I point at something, I adapt to my finger as a pointer. Emotional, expressive movements are those used to express oneself. These movements are the mimic gestures we make, such as gestures of surprise, fright, fear, or joy.

Perhaps you can see how taking hold of an object, handling an instrument, is comparable to dealing with the consonants. The consonants are in a way comparable to instruments. They are the structural elements of language. They are its skeleton. In a dialect, for example, it is primarily the vowels that change. It is particularly the vowels that are pronounced differently. The consonants, you will notice, are much less subject to change. The consonants are more or less the same in different languages, but the vowels are often pronounced in a quite different way. Thus, the vowels can be compared to our expressive movements, our emotional movements, our feelings.

Why is it so important to consider the difference between the two kinds of movement and their relationship to the consonants and vowels? It is important in order to make you realize that we can hear, understand, language by disregarding our own expressions, our own emotions, which by means of our self-movement sense we can observe as movements. We can only listen fully, and hear someone's vowels, when we do not talk at the same time, or make noise, or do something else. We have to put ourselves aside, eliminate ourselves, disregard ourselves. We can erase the musical element in language, therefore, by erasing ourselves. And only when we erase ourselves, set ourselves aside, sacrifice ourselves, are we able to observe in someone else the emotional and formative elements of language. What counts is not that we speak a language ourselves, but that we disregard ourselves and let someone else speak the language.

I already mentioned that we do not form language ourselves. Great cosmic beings form it, through us. It is the archangels who do this. Archangels are not concerned, as are the angels, with the development of individuality. Each human being has his own angel, but not his own archangel. Archangels form groups of human beings, language groups, in which we feel at home, in which we are brought up. You have to look at it this way: When you listen to language, you actually listen through the being of an archangel, who leads a group of people, as it were, and forms them, although not so directly and individually as the angels do, in the language. For language is a formative element. In a language with many consonants, such as, for example, Czech, we can hear even in the structure of that language a different being from the one in a language with many vowels. The whole formative process goes very deeply into the human being. It has much to do with the language he has grown up with.

By immersing ourselves in language this way, we can directly enter the world of the archangel. We then have to abandon ourselves entirely. We have to set aside our own emotions, and take no notice of our own instruments, but only of the instruments of the gods, of the archangels, who are our language spirits or folk spirits, and are removed from us by one more level than the angels. If we have become receptive to this, we notice we do not find it quite so difficult to speak about these supersensible, spiritual senses. It becomes clear to us that with regard to speech we start with hearing – for without ears we can not listen to language – and subsequently erase what we hear and feel: that is language!

Language is a magnificent organic transition from one instrument to the next. These instruments are primarily the feelings and the creative elements of the language spirit, of the archangel, who has made a connection with us.

I will now continue with the *concept sense*. With this, Rudolf Steiner meant to indicate that there is something further beyond hearing language, beyond the ability to recognize language. This is the ability to understand, to comprehend, to picture what is said. Only when we have command of a language and this does not necessarily have to be one's mother tongue – does it become transparent to us when we hear it spoken. We can look right through it. We can follow what is said. This is a delightful experience. We immediately realize that a totally different sort of perception enters our awareness. The words become concepts for us.

Rudolf Steiner said in his philosophical work *Philosophy of Freedom* that we can not express a concept in words. Just try to explain, for instance, what a concept is. You can never really express this in words. Words only indicate that there are such things as concepts.

The interesting thing is, we can never say exactly what we mean. Why not? Because we have a concept of something. We have an idea about something. And where is this idea? In the language? No, it exists on a higher plane. But the trouble is, you need language when you want to pass on the idea to someone else. You have to make up your mind whether you want to say it in English, in French, in Dutch, or in German. And sometimes one language is not enough. Then you have to borrow from another. You have to use a word from another language. In English, for instance, we have no word for the German word *Gestalt*. And a German has no words that express the same as the English phrase 'team work.' This is an English expression that is untranslatable. Sometimes, too, there is a poverty of language in a certain field, and one can not express a certain concept in one's own language. Anthroposophists are all too familiar with this, for Rudolf Steiner, who tried to convey his visions, concepts and thoughts as clearly as possible, did this in German, and sometimes it is difficult to render these concepts in another language. You must all be familiar with this problem in other areas, too. You want to express something you have clearly before you in your mind, an idea you fully grasp, and yet you can not find the words. You sense that there is something else behind the words, something that can not be expressed in words. And if you express it anyway, you end up in a sort of TowerofBabel confusion. You have chosen a certain language, but the idea has no language. It is inexpressible. You can say 'table' in several languages, whichever you want. But what *is* a table? What is the idea 'table'? This is something that lives in a silent world. Ideas live in a silent world. And it is a great experience to become aware that you are able to erase the words too. For you have to reckon with the fact that no one can ever express *exactly* what he wants to express. You only understand someone when you also erase what is said. You have to disregard language. Then you end up not with 'table', 'Tisch' or 'tafel', but with the idea itself.

You see, more and more is erased. In the first place you have to have good hearing, of course, in which the acoustic waves, the vibrations, are erased in order for you to hear. I told you the angel beings are the ones who work in you in connection with this social sense organ. Subsequently, however, you need the help of beings of a still higher hierarchy, the archangels, to erase the musical element in language in order to hear language itself. And you can go further still. At a certain point you can understand a language by erasing the language itself. It becomes transparent to you, so that you rise to the world of the ideas behind language. You then enter directly into a perception someone else has. You do this by erasing language.

Now, the concept sense is opposite the life sense — the sense one uses to perceive one's own constitution, to perceive whether one is feeling unwell or tired, whether one feels pain or hunger, whether one feels listless or full of energy. One observes one's own life body, one's constitution. With the concept sense, on the other hand, one penetrates to ideas. One realizes this has nothing whatsoever to do with one's constitution. On the contrary, when someone has something to say about his or her idea world, it does not depend on one's state of health whether what is said is true or not. One can not say: 'Listen, today the angles of a triangle do not total 180 degrees, for I have a terrible migraine'. No, in order to enter this silent world of ideas, one has to forget about one's life sense. One will need a quite well developed life sense, though, for one can only sacrifice something when there is something to sacrifice.

What do we actually learn through our life sense? We learn about the trials and tribulations of life. I pointed out that we actually welcome effort, that we gladly suffer pain once in a while. We could never penetrate to the truth had we never suffered pain. It is terribly important that the life sense be well trained in youth. If we only spoil our children, they will never suffer pain, and later on they will lack a sense for truth. It is characteristic of an age of ease and prosperity that it tends to suffer from a lack of the sense for truth. What you get then is the sort of thing I will now quote to you from a modern guidance manual. Children are supposed to be told: ... and now you will probably want to know where you come from yourself. From an egg. You have also been an egg. This is the case for all people and animals.' Something like this is soulwrenching to me. For do you know what this says? This is more or less the same as saying: 'Daddy is getting out of the car, Daddy has also been a car'. And this insane untruth must, according to the author of this booklet, be introduced in the first school year. Because this is the truth! The author thinks the stork is nonsense, but not that children have been eggs.

The truth only arises in situations where there is plenty of suffering and grief. That is where the human being develops a sense for truth. I am not saying, let us now go and cause each other a lot of grief so that we can discover the truth. Not at all. But if you ask where truth arises in the human soul, it is always where there has been much suffering. It is not said for nothing that wisdom is crystalized sorrow. It is also very important to let a child have trying experiences, such as having to wait for supper once in a while, having to do things he does not like, or not always getting what he wants. We can not learn to experience a sense for truth, understand someone, discover someone's world of ideas if we have never experienced inner pain. Only when we have learned about physical pain through our life sense can we erase this feeling, this experience, and feel pain when someone does not speak the truth. I am not talking about moral truth. The author of that guidance booklet means well one hundred percent. She is not out to pull the wool over those children's eyes. She says it with one hundred percent conviction – Christian conviction, I would almost say. But what she says is painful because there is no truth in it. It defies the simplest logic. Unfortunately, fewer and fewer people have a sense for truth, which is, in fact, something we must develop more and more.

When we talk about the world of ideas, which world do we actually mean? What is this world in which all that is externally audible is erased, where words do not exist, where language is unimportant, where only concepts exist? It has to be a world in which the language spirits are of no importance either. Rudolf Steiner says in this respect that we owe the concept sense to a higher being who works through people in a helping way. Just as the angels help us to perceive sound, and the archangels help us to distinguish language, so are we dealing with the *Spirit of Humanity* here. We are really dealing directly here with the *Christ Being*.

You might want to stop and think about this — that when the world becomes totally silent in the world of ideas, we are connected with each other through that which is universally human. We find something within ourselves that connects all of us with each other, something that can not be expressed in language, but is behind the expression, and lives in all of us in the form of ideas, of concepts. And in this life of concepts we find the first bridge to the Christ. This is where we meet the Christ as a cosmic being, as a third dimension beyond the angels and the archangels. I do not mean that we do this in a senti-mental way, but in a way that is concerned with the things that are right in front of us, things about which we can have a common understanding.

The concept sense, therefore, arises in a twofold way: by erasing the life sense and simultaneously sacrificing something of ourselves. One can say: the concept sense functions through the life sense, but by refraining from using the latter. This is a difficult concept. We always tend to think that when something is *not* said, it is not there, it is gone. But saying 'no' to something here and now means that a sense is opened on the other side. I hope you can grasp this more or less; we are obviously dealing with something here that is quite hard to put into words. What I mean is that when we keep silent about something, it is there all the same; in spite of dismissing something, denying it, ignoring it, it still exists elsewhere. Each non—reaction on one side has an opposite reaction on the other side. Once we get familiar with this idea, we begin to realize how practice during youth — making an effort to achieve something, giving something of oneself — always calls forth another kind of capacity later on, a capacity for sacrifice, which in the life sense can advance to the point where the human being can gradually come to know the being who binds us together when people listen to one another. In this connection you can appreciate a positive aspect of our culture, namely that there is a great urge not only to read and study, but also to form groups of people. People like to speak with each other, indeed to have endless discussions! There is a profound motivation behind this tendency, and that is that we want to listen *behind* each other's words, for that is where, indeed, we meet the representative of humanity, the Christ. This is possible for each of us if we engage our life sense and concept sense.

This is connected with the Bull (*Taurus*, ♉). Do you realize what is so miraculous about the bull, the cow, or bovines in general? It is a very strong animal of which everything is usable: its meat, its skin, its hair, its horns. Even the manure is usable. Just try and name any part of the bovine that is not usable in daily life. In short, the bull is the ultimate sacrificial animal. This is what is contained in this sign of the zodiac in concordance with the concept sense. We are truly dealing here with the sense that sacrifices everything that is present in the human being, as it were. It is not, as the life sense is, concerned only with ourself, with our constitution, warning us when something goes wrong. No, it is the sense that lets us put ourselves totally aside in order to find out what someone else says, what someone else means. The great sacrifice, of which the Bull is the sign, is contained in the concept sense. That is why it has become the unifying element for all of us.

And now I will return to the speech sense for a moment, for I can now tell you why the speech sense is related to the Twins (*Gemini*, ♊). What are you doing when you listen to someone? By way of language you are trying to penetrate his idea world. And in conversation one may notice how, as the listener, one sometimes grasps the idea of the other so well that one actually succeeds much better in finding the right words than the speaker. One is able to supplement the words of the speaker so well that he or she says: 'Yes, the way you said it is actually how I meant it'. When we listen to someone, we can sometimes see the struggle to make the inaudible world audible. This is a creative element. When we hear someone speak, we may notice how he is creatively engaged, trying to bring a higher world down to earth. This has to do with the constellation of the Twins. You often see the Twins depicted as two children at play. This really is a very appropriate way of representing this constellation. For it is the zodiacal sign of the creative human being. And only children are really creative. Even in adulthood it is only the child within that is creative.

Philosophy is also a form of play. It is a creative game — the very serious game of finding the exact words to express an idea. Philosophy and poetry are closely related. The philosopher renders his creation in philosophical terms, and the poet in a poetic form. The poet also struggles. He has the same problem. There is something higher that, through language, has to be given an earthly manifestation. Unfortunately, a specific language has to be chosen for poetry. Perhaps the art of movement called eurythmy will eventually give us an experience of speech without language. Maybe a language, and the idea behind it, will be made so explicit, so real, that we will begin to experience the 'silent language'. For the present we have not got that far.

Following the language sense and the concept — or thought sense there is, finally, a last sense to be dealt with, which is the *Ego Sense*. Rudolf Steiner did not mean with this that you can say 'I' to yourself or that you experience yourself as an individual, but that you become aware of someone else as an 'I', that another person you are talking to, whom you are dealing with, is an individual. We know that when someone speaks, we do not only hear sound. Neither do you hear only that someone speaks a particular language. Even what is meant by what is said is not the only thing you hear. You also become aware that it is *he* or *she* who means something by it, at least if you have developed your ego sense to some extent. For there is an enormous difference between one person saying something and another saying the same thing. This is a very peculiar, but immensely important experience. Unfortunately, in our time this ability is becoming more and more ignored. It is not considered so important anymore *who* says something. As long as someone speaks the truth it is already considered quite an achievement, never mind who it is who speaks the truth. But this, in fact, is the only thing that really counts. You see, it is pretty hard to say anything original. And all too often it turns out that what people say is only a repetition of what someone else said — it could even be a distorted repetition. It is very important, therefore, to find out who says what, and whether it is really said out of the speaker's own conviction. If it is, even a truth that has been around for ages can take on a new meaning, while a truth not discovered by the speaker personally — a truth repeated from another source — can never be very inspiring. That is why we must learn to become sensitive to this organ of perception, to this sense for perceiving someone's individuality. You may find that when someone says: 'This is what we are going to do', your reaction is that there is no way you are going to go along, but that when someone else says it, you simply can not be kept away.

The mystery we can experience with respect to the ego sense is: Who is behind the words, behind the idea? You often find yourself wondering whether something being said has political overtones or is meant honestly. Does the speaker stand behind it? Can we count on him, yes or no? This is something we can discover by means of the ego sense. But we have to make very sure that we do not allow our ego sense to be annihilated by political propaganda, or by the halftruths often spewed out by the media, or by advertising, sloganeering, and promotions, or by puffery or slanted information in the newspapers, and so on. If we are on the alert for this, we may become aware that although everyone has certain tasks in life and has to utilize a certain language and certain ideas in order to carry out these tasks, we have to penetrate to the I of those who are in the forefront in order to discover whether we should let ourselves be guided, or whether we are being led down the garden path.

We need the ego sense for this. The ego sense is present in everyone, although it is under attack all the time.

We immediately notice when we talk to someone that the other is an I, an individuality. We know we are not talking to a doll or to an animal. We meet on the basis of I to I. Just think of the difference it makes whether it is another person who steps on your toes, or a dog. It makes quite a difference. You feel annoyed when another person steps on your toes. You are not annoyed by a dog stepping on your toes; a dog doesn't know any better. Of course it doesn't. It hasn't got an I. But a person has. We always seem to notice most intensely that someone else has an I in a fight or a disagreement. In a fight there is never any doubt about it. As long as we agree with someone, we can afford to pay more attention to ourselves, to our own ideas, but as soon as we get into a conflict, we meet the I in the other for sure. For we can only be angered or insulted by another I. This is the funny thing about the senses; we often notice them most acutely as a result of negative experiences.

I told you that in language we are dealing with vowels and consonants. When I pronounce a word, for instance, 'plant', there is an organic sequence of different instruments one after the other, linked in a beautiful organic sound. When we perceive an idea, an inexpressible idea — not the word 'plant, but the idea 'plant' — what do we really perceive? Pretty obvious, is it not? It is an entire musical score, a beautiful sonata. And the idea behind 'table', 'Tisch', 'tafel', is another musical score — a different world again. Each idea is an entire world on its own. We need an even more absurd mental picture than when we penetrate the language world. We do not merely hear a sequence of instruments, no, it is as if you hear a sequence of different compositions: a piece by Mozart, a piece by Beethoven, a piece by Gounod. And what do we do when we hear someone utter a sentence? A sentence consists of many compositions, which are themselves gathered up in a composition, because this sentence does not consist of separate words, of separate ideas, but is an organic totality. It is truly astonishing how in a sentence these compositions can be heard one after another at an incredibly rapid pace — time, obviously, is irrelevant here. It is like a series of concerts, as it were, a composition of a super-concert in which everything is brought together. I hope you can make some sense of this image, for with it I hope to be able to illustrate to you that when we listen to someone, when we meet the I of someone else, when we use our ego sense, we actually end up with the 'conductor' of all these compositions that are being performed for us.

The ego sense comes about by ignoring the tones when someone speaks, ignoring the speaker's use of a certain language, ignoring, even, what he says, but being sensitive to whether he stands behind what he says, whether his being really means what he says, or, in fact, does not mean it. Just as there are beautiful and ugly colours, so we also experience a demonic element when the speaker is not fully behind what he says, when he is a traitor to the cause. This is the I element of the other. We have to make a much greater sacrifice to perceive this than we do for the concept sense. We first have to use the sense of touch for this, which is the opposite, within ourselves. I told you that in our sense of touch we close ourselves off from the world. With touch we do not enter the world, but we confront the world, while we wall ourselves in. This is what is needed here, for in order to see through the I of the other we should not start from a void. We first have to become well 'clad'. We do this with our sense of touch. It puts us inside our own armour. And with our ego sense we have to undo this again. We do not do this consciously, of course. That is impossible, for even though we say 'I', and feel ourselves as an 'I' in our physical body, our I has not truly incarnated at all. We experience it as if it had; we even experience it as if it were within us, but this is only because of our sense of touch. The I is not something that occupies our body like a dwelling, with definite boundaries. That is nonsense. We only experience it in that way because our sense of touch links our I with our body. And what we have to do is to let go of the tie with our own I, forget about it. In this way we meet the I of another person. And because this does not take place consciously, it is spontaneous. We do not have to be adults for this to take place. Small children meet the I of other people right away, through eye contact — with the mother, and with others in their surroundings. But we do have to sustain and nourish this ability, which is why touch is so important.

In my first talk I explained that it is not the same whether an infant feels the mother's breast or a bottle. I spoke about the intimacy of touch, and how, because of it, we create distance between ourselves and the world, how it causes us to confront the world, but at the same time with the deep conviction that we have a connection with the world.

This deeply religious element, this transcendental element, has to do with touch. All that a child encounters by way of touch has at that very moment a deep truth for it. It is not at all the same thing whether the child wears pullovers of wool or of acrylic. It is not the same thing whether this pullover has been knitted by grandmother or has been manufactured. There is an immense difference. For even if the latter might look better, not a single thread of love or warmth has been knitted into it. Everything a child experiences through touch lays the foundation for the ego sense. It makes a great deal of difference whether a child plays with plastic toys or with living materials, such as wood.

You will discover that you become a materialist as soon as you get into anthroposophy. Only then do you become a true materialist, in the sense that you become more discerning with respect to matter. Rudolf Steiner was not one to draw us only into the world of angels and archangels. He pointed out that it is in the earthly element, in matter, that the deepest secrets are contained. This surely is the last thing we will come to understand: matter, our mother-ground.

Matter, in fact, is of the greatest importance for a child. What does it come into contact with? For only to the extent that those responsible for its upbringing have paid attention to this, will a child be able to penetrate through the ideas to the inner being of others when he has become an adult, when he stands in the world as an independent individual. We can only have these encounters, this penetration to the being of others, by erasing a well-developed sense of touch. We have to erase entirely the fact that we are individualities. Because we are then no longer directed inward, we are able to break through to the other. We break through all of the physical nature of the other. When we perceive the I of the other, we no longer see the physical body. This happens not only by way of our hearing; we can often also see this immediately in someone's gaze.

I hope you now appreciate why I had to deal with the senses as a composition. We can not deal with them separately or in an arbitrary sequence − no more than you can play music without knowing where the notes are on the keyboard. A piece-meal study of the senses is useless; everything has an amazing coherence. You do not develop the ego sense by a lot of contact with other people, by seeing important personalities, by looking at people on television a lot. No, the ego sense is developed because we have learned to make a distinction between wool, cotton, and synthetic pullovers. Not so long ago, everybody knew that the sense of touch is of immense importance for babies. The way children were clothed was a question approached with a great deal of care, and whether the child looked nice and pretty was of no account. That is why babies used to be put into a bunting bag. This helped them to push with their little legs. When they did, they felt the pressure on their shoulders from the tension of the shoulder straps. So, a bunting bag should never be too large. Such a garment makes a lot more sense for small infants than, for instance, 'cute' wide, cuffed trousers, made of denim. Clothing for children has nowadays become a social problem − one that is mainly of the parents' making − while the important thing, really, is to know what is good for the child's development.

In his lectures about the senses, Rudolf Steiner described how we actually go on the defensive inwardly, how we inwardly resist the I of someone else, when we speak with someone or listen to someone intensively. This is because we feel that the other − whose I is just as important as our own, since he or she is also a human being − attacks our own I, in a way, takes possession of it. In the eighth lecture of Steiner's lecture cycle

Study of Man, which he gave in 1919 for the faculty of the first Waldorf School in Stuttgart on the occasion of the school's founding, he had this to say: 'When you confront someone, the following takes place. For a brief period you observe the other; he makes an impression on you. This impression has a disturbing effect on you inwardly; you feel that the other, who is in effect of the same kind as yourself, seems to attack you. The result is that you immediately take up a defensive position, that you resist this attack, that inwardly you become aggressive towards him. Then your aggression diminishes, and ceases altogether; as a result, the other can once again make an impression on you. This gives you time to increase your aggression and inwardly you make an aggressive gesture again. The aggression fades again, and the other can make another impression, etc. This is the interaction that takes place between two people when perceiving the I of the other: surrender to the other — inner resistance; surrender — resistance; sympathy — antipathy; sympathy — antipathy. I am not talking about feelings now, but only about the perception of the other. The soul vibrates in sympathy — antipathy, sympathy — antipathy, sympathy — antipathy.'

You can understand that you always have to be alert in your dealings with others. Leaders of cults know this. They misuse this knowledge by taking possession of another at an instant when the other's I is momentarily weak. This is why cult leaders are often so afraid of their followers' having too much contact with the outside world. They fear that their followers' natural feeling that a human being can not stand it when another takes total possession of him, immersing in him totally, will reawaken. Conversations and interaction with others must always be a positive inner battle with those others. The perception of the I in others is a very wakeful process. It is something in which we always need to be completely awake spiritually, a capacity first acquired physically, by a sound development of our touch, and subsequently by erasing it again.

This is the Ram (*Aries*, ♈) principle. The constellation of the Ram presents an image of the great battle we have with the other, without losing sight of each other. It is the battle in which we confront the other again and again, absorbing the other, and erasing him again in order to regain inner space, to prime ourselves again in order to confront the other again, while leaving the I of the other free. For this is how it has to be in a conversation. In a conversation we should never go into a trance, never lose our I, for this would be unhealthy. On the other hand, we should never convince anyone forcibly, for just as our own I has to remain free, so do we also have to leave the I of the other free.

And this brings me right away to the two great errors we continually make. On the one hand we continually allow ourselves to be seduced by impressive advertising slogans, etc. And, on the other hand, we continually try to impose our own opinions or convictions on others. These are both tremendous attacks on the I — in the one instance on our own I, and in the other on the I of someone else. We are often so convinced of being right that we do not consider the opinion of others; we do not allow them to judge for themselves. You all know how often it happens in meetings and conferences that we arrive at a certain conclusion, and the next time around we totally ignore these conclusions. Well, this is a blessing, indeed! For sound judgment is a very difficult business. A judgment arises wherever people meet. For even though there has been this meeting where a momentous conclusion, a solid conclusion, has been arrived at (particularly if there were many men present), still, one has discussions in the hallways, one meets others, one thinks the matter over again, one sleeps on it, or, in fact, has a restless night over it, and the next day one sees it all differently, for one has met a person with an I. This changes one's opinion. And this is quite healthy. For instead of agreeing not to talk about the matter any further, simply because an agreement has been reached, one that should be adhered to, it is important that people deploy their ego sense.

But you can appreciate how we can time and again be overwhelmed by another's opinion, by another I. This is the other side, and this requires the Ram principle. We have to break through the wall, but then we have to withdraw again and others have to be allowed to find their place within us. This is pre-eminently the Ram principle.

You can see that our higher senses need considerable further development!

In closing I want to leave you with something in the way of an exercise, as an example you can play with. Our senses are *capacities* of our being. And I mean by this that these are capacities that are active within us, capacities we can develop. In the course of our development (and this already begins in the embryonic stage) these capacities become active especially in certain parts of our organism. The capacity for vision, for instance, creates the eye as an 'instrument', and the capacity for hearing creates the organ of hearing.

When you listen to an orchestra, you should try, after a while, to take notice only of the flute. Do you do this with your ears? Of course you need your ears for this, but which sense has the capability to concentrate on a particular aspect? It is sight, of course. You can only pay special attention to the flute, you can only hear the flute in particular, when you 'look through your ears'. This is a capability we humans have, namely to start using a sense somewhere other than where it is normally active.

Thus you can also 'hear' with your eyes. You can observe in an art gallery how people look at paintings. Do you know what people do when they want to take in the beauty of a painting? They do not look straight at the painting, but they step back a few paces, turn their head this way and that; and they prefer to have silence. They do this because they want to take in the harmony of the painting, or, indeed, its dissonance. They want to 'hear' it. If we could do this only with our eyes, why would we look from a distance? Why would we turn our head, turn our ear to the painting? In fact, we want to hear, with our eyes, how harmonious the totality is. And we do this every day. As soon as we enter the realm of beauty, we can not observe it only with our soul. We need a spiritual sense. We have to hear. 'Does this painting have anything to say to me?' 'What language does it speak?' 'What is the thought behind it?' These are the sort of questions we seek to answer.

Perhaps you know the beautiful painting *The Sower*, by Van Gogh. You see half atmosphere, half earth. On the horizon is the sun. And this sun shines only via the head of the sower, as it were. In any case, we can see how the head of the sower 'shines'. Is this not a great composition? Is it not a magnificent idea that lies behind this, namely that man can only sow in the earth if he is connected with the sun? This is a composition that almost guarantees that our concept sense will become active. We also experience how we hear the painting as soon as we perceive the harmony. This is how the senses enhance each other so wonderfully.

I could give many examples like this. I told you how important it is first to develop smell externally in order to experience good and evil. You will perhaps agree with me that nowadays we almost always have to hold our nose when we look at picture books for children. When we see all these caricatures that are inflicted on children, does it not smell pretty awful? Don't you think all these things children take in with their eyes must be disastrous for their sense of smell and taste? And what about the garbage on television, such as cartoons? We do not even notice any longer how many grotesque images rush across the screen, accompanied by a gross misuse of the human voice. This complete absence of awareness is the result of habit formed over years and a kind of narcosis. Children, even those less than a year old, are confronted with this as something 'educational' – you have to move with the times, right!

The most fatal aspect of this is the serials. Every sensible person, surely, knows that it is the repetition – the same story unchanged for a month – that is true nourishment for a child. The irony is, that is why children like these insipid commercials so much. At least there is some repetition!

How can people be under the illusion that this apparatus has anything to do with education? Even in small auditoriums a microphone is deemed necessary for a children's party – otherwise it is not 'in'.

It would be of great significance if we really took our senses as our teachers and allowed one sense to work through another. This would allow us to internalize our sense of smell, for instance, with which we determine whether something is clean or unclean. Some of this ability could then be used in other senses. Only then would we learn to discover that a drawing can be brilliantly clever, and yet utterly tasteless and immoral.

We are justifiably worried about pollution of the earth, the water, and the atmosphere. Pollution of the senses has unfortunately not yet become a recognized concept. May these considerations help that come about.

I hope I gave you homework for the rest of your lives, and may the guiding principle in this be a deep respect for the twelve senses.

Synopsis

On the following pages, some of the main points regarding the contents of the lectures have be represented in a schematic form.

Schematic representation

Groups	The twelve senses	Associated signs of the zodiac
Physical senses	1. *Touch*	Libra (♎)
(Directed at own physical body)	2. *Life sense*	Scorpio (♏)
	3. *Self-movement sense*	Sagittarius (♐)
	4. *Balance*	Capricorn (♑)
Soul Senses	5. *Smell*	Aquarius (♒)
(Relation of man to the world)	6. *Taste*	Pisces (♓)
	7. *Vision*	Virgo (♍)
	8. *Temperature sense (warmth sense)*	Leo (♌)
Spiritual, Social Senses	9. *Hearing*	Cancer (♋)
(directed inward, revealing latent element)	10. *Language sense (word, speech sense)*	Gemini (♊)
	11. *Conceptual sense (thought sense)*	Taurus (♉)
	12. *Ego sense*	Aries (♈)

of the twelve senses

Experience	Spriritual source
Physical body	. . .
Ether (life) body	Spirit man
Astral body (Expressive— and adaptive forms)	Life spirit
I (Opposing gravity)	Spirit self
Physical matter (Direct)(Instincts)	Consciousness soul (Willing)(Morality) (Judgment: good/bad)
Ether (life) substance (Dissolved)(fluid)	Intellectual/mind soul (Feeling)(Quality) (Judgment: healthy/ unhealthy)
Astral substance (Sun, light)	Sentient soul (Thinking) (Freedom of choice)
Atmosphere/air/warmth	Archetypal sense/ astrality (Warmth/interest)
Physical (Solid matter)	Angels (Social element)
Ether (Spirit constitution of the other)	Archangels
Astral (Inner sun, truth of the other)	Christ being (Spirit of humanity)
I (Being of the other)	. . .

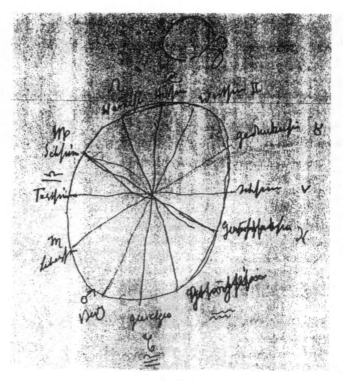

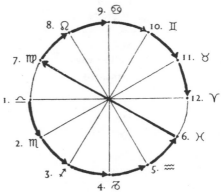

The twelve senses as six polarities

1. TOUCH Determining one's boundaries	12. EGO SENSE Breaking through another's boundaries
2. LIFE SENSE Growth and decay of own constitution	11. CONCEPTUAL SENSE Truth/falsehood in spirit of another
3. SELF-MOVEMENT SENSE Handling/expressing oneself through body	10. LANGUAGE SENSE How another handles/expresses the spirit: through speech
4. BALANCE Gravitational orientation	9. HEARING Rising to the spirit of matter
5. SMELL Emptying oneself and being filled (materially)	8. TEMPERATURE SENSE Pouring out into the world with one's interest (non-materially)
6. TASTE Controlling the ponderable: what forms my body (microcosm)	7. VISION Experiencing the imponderable (effect of sunlight) in the macrocosm

These six polarities can be recognized in a drawing in Rudolf Steiner's note book:
– The four physical senses are opposite the four spiritual senses;
– The four soul senses are opposite in pairs.

Through an understanding of these six polarities, one can also get a clear picture of the relation between the twelve senses and the twelve signs of the zodiac, especially when we place the signs of the zodiac in a circle in their mutual relationships. On the opposite page is a reproduction of Rudolf Steiner's sketch (as it was printed in *Beiträge zur Rudolf Steiner Gesamtausgabe, nr. 58/59, 1977*), with a more elaborate diagram based on this sketch below it.

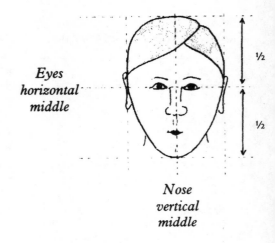

*Eyes
horizontal
middle*

*Nose
vertical
middle*

Smell:

Temperature sense:

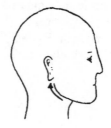

The two polarities for the four soul senses

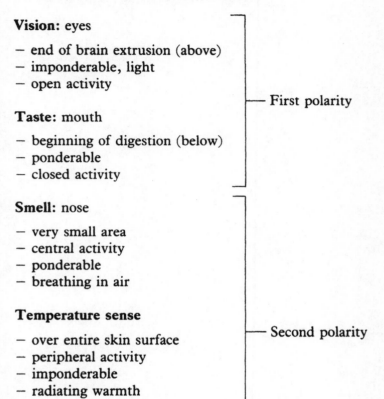

Vision: eyes

– end of brain extrusion (above)
– imponderable, light
– open activity

Taste: mouth

– beginning of digestion (below)
– ponderable
– closed activity

—— First polarity

Smell: nose

– very small area
– central activity
– ponderable
– breathing in air

Temperature sense

– over entire skin surface
– peripheral activity
– imponderable
– radiating warmth

—— Second polarity

Hearing as the first spiritual sense

Hearing

Internalizing process (social process) during development:
– backwards
– inwards
– becoming still
– from metabolic/limb system (jaw) and breathing system (gill slit)

Appendix I

On Coming to Our Senses
John Davy

Every morning, I wake up. This simple phrase describes a mysterious – and in my case rather gradual – process. I wake up first to sounds – birdsong, the newspaper being shoved through the letter-box, a small boy playing trains in the next room. Next comes awareness of warmth (or cold if the blankets have fallen off), and of position and weight; cramp if I have been lying awkwardly, the pleasures of moving and stretching. Sometimes smells come next – especially if bacon is being fried downstairs – and perhaps a dawning awareness of hunger. Only then may I open my eyes, a bit dazzled at first, gradually beginning to 'see'. Getting out of bed, washing, shaving, dressing, breakfast, and the first conversations of the day continue the process.

On some mornings, I may feel 'all there' within a few minutes of waking; on other, more reluctant days, it may be well after breakfast before I feel fully able to cope with the world. But however this extraordinary metamorphosis of consciousness occurs, as it has done regularly and without fail since the day I was born, it marks a daily gateway to life on earth, to all conscious relations with nature and with other people.

Waking up is deeply involved with a sphere of human nature which is easily taken for granted – the scenes, and the perceptions they offer. If we want to wake someone up, we switch on a light, call out, touch him, shake him by the shoulder, or as a last resort dribble cold water on his face from a sponge. In other words, we stimulate his senses of sight, hearing, touch and movement, warmth and cold. We bring him – sometimes a bit roughly – 'to his senses'. Wherever we may be during sleep, the senses bring us down to earth to an awareness of ourselves, inhabiting bodies and surveying a surrounding world.

Once awake, and if we begin to attend more carefully to the role of the senses in everyday life, we find that they are essential to thought, feeling and action. Most of our thoughts have a content derived from past sense-experiences – memories and the like. Our desires demand satisfaction through the senses (normal people are not content to imagine a steak or a symphony; they insist on tasting the one and hearing the other, in reality). Our actions and physical skills depend on healthy senses of balance, movement and touch (as the drunk whose senses are disordered by alcohol may discover rather painfully). A damaged or destroyed sense can be far more crippling than loss of a limb.

If we reflect on these experiences, leaving aside all theories about sense-organs and sense-perception that we may have learnt, we can become aware that throughout our waking hours the senses are providing a kind of *nourishment* – a content for our thoughts, sensations for our feelings, an essential support for our actions. The most physically massive kind of nourishment that we need to live properly in our bodies and on earth is the food we supply to our stomachs and digestive system. A second, and finer kind of nourishment is the air we breathe into our lungs, so that the blood is supplied with oxygen. Without adequate supplies of either of these, we grow faint and may die. But through our senses, which are linked through the central nervous system to our brain, we are nourished in a still finer way. We are supplied, so to speak, with 'light' – the light of day. Without this nourishment we cannot wake up properly.

In preparation for manned space flights, experiments were made in the United States with volunteers who underwent almost complete 'sensory deprivation'. They floated in water at blood heat, immobile, surrounded by silence, wearing goggles which admitted only a dim, diffuse light or no light at all, and soft gloves to damp out touch. Most volunteers quickly fell asleep at first. But later they would wake up, and in some cases be gradually overcome by uncontrolled fantasies, hallucinations, or disordered perceptions of their own bodies (feeling, for example, that a foot or a leg had grown to an enormous size and was floating away from the rest of the body). These experiments showed vividly how essential a free flow of normal sense-experience is for a healthy day-time consciousness.

Further exploration of our own sense-experience shows that this 'nourishment' reaches us as a variety of distinct sensations, which before we begin to weave thoughts around them, have the nature of pure 'activities': warmth, colour, sound, movement, etc. Each of these qualities of activity is differentiated within itself (we experience a whole range of colours, of tones, etc.), but offers a distinct realm or mode of experience (defined physiologically, of course, by the functioning of a particular sense-organ or set of organs). If we contemplate the senses in this way, we may begin to understand what Rudolf Steiner meant when he once described the senses as 'well-springs'.[1] These wells are filled with what I have called the 'light of day' from sources lying outside our direct daytime experience.[2] The human being, Steiner remarks, dips into these springs to meet the needs of his soul, his inner life.

Steiner goes on, both here and in other books and lectures, to describe how there are really twelve of these 'well-springs' flowing into our waking lives, twelve distinct modes of sense-experience, or, more simply that we have twelve senses. Of some of these, such as sound, sight, warmth, etc., we are vividly aware. Of others we are barely aware unless they go wrong, notably balance and movement (which textbooks usually call the proprioceptive and kinaesthetic senses). A few are not at present clearly recognised at all.

The twelve are: touch, life movement, balance, smell, taste, sight, warmth, hearing, thought, word and 'I'. Of these, eight are clearly recognised in modern textbooks. A ninth, the sense of 'life', is less clearly defined, but in Steiner's terms is responsible for our sensations of general bodily 'well-being' (or ill-being), as well as the physical component of the sense of pain.[3] The final three: 'word', 'thought' and 'I' (By which Steiner means the direct perception of the 'I' of another human being), are not to be found in any text-books. I shall have more to say about them below.

So far, I have described these twelve well-springs as bringers of a kind of nourishment for our healthy day-consciousness. But now we must recognise that the senses also bring problems which have had profound effects on human life throughout history. These problems are of two main kinds: problems of morality and problems of knowledge.

In the East, and in the past, men were much concerned with the role of the senses in moral behaviour. They can tempt to indulgence, egotism, excessive 'attachment' to the pleasures of this world. Again and again, ascetic and puritan teachings have arisen, urging men to 'purify' or even as far as possible to deny their senses - or rather, to deny satisfaction to those desires which can only be stilled temporarily with the help of the senses. The pleasures of this world, men have repeatedly been told, are vain, illusory, and divert the soul from its true path, which should be to seek a Divine and unfallen world by withdrawing from our daytime world.

Nowadays, there are only faint echoes of such moral debates in scientific cultures, although many people probably feel vaguely guilty after excessive bouts of indulgence in food, drink, sex or generally luxurious living. But the issue is still with us, in a new, unexpected and still barely recognised guise. It lives, in fact, in the problem of economic growth, and the struggle for 'higher standards of living'.

Of course there are millions of people struggling for a higher standard for simple reasons of health, strength and minimum human dignity. But in the 'advanced' countries, vast numbers of people consume quantities of food, goods and services far greater than they need for sufficiency. The essential product offered by many consumer industries consists of sense-experiences; and the true consumers are the insatiable human appetites attached to them magnified by advertising and elaborate forms of stimulation. When salesmen are taught 'don't sell the steak, sell the sizzle', they are acknowledging that their real customers are our senses of hearing (plus sight, taste and smell), and not our stomachs (where we are more or less unconscious, except when we have indigestion).

What an Eastern teacher in the past might have called excessive attachment to self and to earthly illusion, we might call addiction: enslavement to appetites and sensations which have got out of hand, so that we are no longer nourished and supported, but made dependent and ill. The very phrase 'a slave to such and such' expresses our direct experience that our true selves are not identical with these sensations and desires, but subject to and entangled in them. Monsters can lurk in our well-springs, and drag us in to drown.

The second problem in which the senses are deeply involved is that of knowledge. I have assumed that the senses enable us to 'know the world', that they bring us the true light of day. 'Seeing is believing', we say. If I am not sure whether I can 'believe my eyes', I may pinch myself to make sure that I am awake and not dreaming. If I *am* properly awake, the implication is, then I can and must believe my eyes.

Nevertheless, Eastern teachers and religions have frequently held what the senses reveal is Maya – illusion, a veil over a different reality. In a new guise, this issue has re-emerged in modern times in science and philosophy, as we have come to believe that ultimate reality is something other than what our senses reveal to our normal consciousness. We do not see the atoms, particles, or waves of which the universe is supposed to consist. The experiences conveyed by the senses are held to be 'subjective' and therefore not to be naively trusted. In very recent times, the notion that our senses hide rather than reveal a more profound reality has also been revived in connection with drug experiences. Under the influence of mescalin, Aldous Huxley believed that 'doors of perception', which are normally closed, began to open.

At the same time there is a wider social problem, a kind of companion to the problem of growth and excessive consumption, which goes by the name of 'alienation'. This word has come to be used very broadly to describe a kind of inner loneliness and isolation, a sense of being 'out of touch' with the world, as stranger among strangers who can never really meet each other properly, and who are not perhaps to be wholly trusted. In political life, the problem of trust has loomed very large in recent years, and there is often a growing sense of a discrepancy between the public 'image' of a person and the private 'reality', hidden but perhaps fundamentally inaccessible, behind a mask.

Such problems point to a kind of illness or disorder in the sphere of sense-perception, whose true function, as we have seen, is to lead us into a healthy waking consciousness in which we 'come to our senses', and can thereby live properly in the world. 'Alienation' points to a kind of dream state persisting into waking life, and inadequate 'coming down to earth', whereas greed and addiction point to an opposite extreme, in which we become frantic consumers of sense-experiences to feed insatiable drives and desires.

These social disorders point to the need for a kind of therapy for the senses, a therapy which will depend on a deeper understanding of the twelve realms of sense-experience that Rudolf Steiner describes. 'The I', he once remarked, 'moves among the circle of the twelve senses as the sun moves among the signs of the Zodiac'. We have some direct awareness of this in the simple capacity to 'attend' to one mode of sense-experience or another – to be particularly awake in our hearing, for example, or in the sense of smell. When we are deeply absorbed in one mode of sense-experience, the others retire into the background. but if we attend in turn to the various senses Steiner describes, we shall discover that the circle is differentiated in many ways – it has a complex anatomy and structure.

One kind of distinction to which Rudolf Steiner drew attention[4] is between six more 'inward' senses – touch, life, movement, balance, taste, smell – and the remaining six which tend to take us more out of ourselves, so to speak – sight, warmth, hearing, word, thought, 'I'. In the first four of the first set, we are clearly concerned in perceptions of our own bodies. *Touch* defines for us the bodily boundary of the skin; *life* the harmony or disharmony of our body's contents; *movement* allows us to be aware of the motions of muscles and joints; *balance* allows us to perceive how our weight is disposed in space. When we attend to the sensations conveyed by these senses, we are turned inwards to our own bodies. Here we are seldom troubled by distrust of our perceptions. We use touch as a kind of ultimate test of reality; one does not argue about a sense of bodily discomfort – if we don't feel well, there is no room for doubt.

Nor do we ever question the trustworthiness of our senses of movement and balance. Here, quite particularly, we find a sureness and security in our relation to our own bodies.

Taste and smell begin to relate us to aspects of nature outside our own organism. Nevertheless, these senses function only when we draw fine vapours deep into our nose, or dissolve something on the tongue. We also react in a particularly personal way to tastes and smells, the latter conjuring up personal memories and associations, the former often being involved with strong personal preferences. A person's 'taste' in food, drink, clothes, literature, etc., is a very individual matter.

Through these six senses we are strongly attached to our own bodies, and in taste and smell are 'consumers' of products of nature. It is through these senses, more particularly, that we are prone to indulgence in 'sensuality' and greed. On the other hand, the healthy function of these senses is the basis for secure, 'down-to-earth' waking consciousness, and it is through these senses that we know most directly and intimately, through knowing them in our own body, the 'primary qualities' of the earth – weight, movement, solidity, and so on. In early childhood, as we learn to manage our bodies and move around in the physical world, it is these senses in particular which serve us as we learn to become earth citizens.

Our whole orientation begins to change with the senses of sight (which in this context should be understood more specifically as the sense of colour), and warmth. Here we experience a kind of 'breathing' with the surrounding world, and the certainties of the more body-oriented senses begin to dissolve. Colour and warmth are most often quoted in popular text books as proof that all sense-perception is 'subjective'. If we emerge into a mild day from the cold room or from a hot room, the same outside air feels warm or cool. So we cannot trust our senses, we are told. This is revealed as complete nonsense as soon as we realise that these senses show us *relationships* – and show them with great precision. Our sense of warmth in effect tells us whether we are losing or gaining warmth from our surroundings, or from an object we are touching. Colour perception also brings us an experience of colour as a relationship between the hue of an object and the ambient illumination (This is why, when we buy clothes, we try to inspect them both by daylight and by artificial light).

These two senses are a kind of bridge to a world *other than* ourselves (in so far as we identify our 'self' with percepts of our own organism). With hearing, as Rudolf Steiner often described, we begin to enter into a kind of 'inwardness' of what is around us.

You see a vase in a room. It may not be clear to the eye whether it is made of metal, clay or stone – but tap it with a finger and you will know at once. The sound allows you to hear right into the matter of which it is made (this fact is widely exploited in engineering, where ultrasonic vibrations are used to detect flaws in metal structures, on the same principle as a crack in a bell is instantly audible as a flawed tone). The eye shows us a bird or a cow from outside; but the sounds uttered by these animals convey something of their inner joys and sufferings. Most far-reaching of all, of course, is the entry into the 'inwardness' of another human being which begins when he opens his mouth and speaks.

Hearing, as Steiner describes it, is the first of four senses which play the most crucial role in human relationships. The others are the sense of word, thought and 'I'. Steiner sometimes described these four senses as a kind of turning inside out of the four 'body ' senses of balance, movement, life and touch. This is a theme on which much research will be needed in the future, and all I can do here is to point to a few phenomena which seen to me suggestive for further study.

The sense of hearing, as we all know, is anatomically closely associated with the sense of balance in the ear. But I am here concerned not so much with the anatomy and physiology of these senses as with exploring and comparing the sense-experiences themselves. Here it is worth noting that the sense of balance leads us into security of stance in physical space, while hearing leads us most strongly 'out of ourselves' into a totally different kind of 'space' which is essentially 'weightless': we can observe this most strongly when listening to music. If we could trust our senses, we would realise that a symphony is not *in* the air waves of the concert hall, but that we perceive ther music *through* these waves, and with the help of our ears can reach directly into a reality of which the air waves are merely a bearer, not the cause.

The sense of word – or more precisely the sense of speech-sounds – reveals to us the 'sculpture', the gestures, made by a speaker's larynx, tongue and lips, which shape a stream of sound into the forms of vowels and consonants. These forms are composed by the speaker into a kind of 'dance' – something between gesture and music – a sequence of sounds which is characteristic of the particular language he is using. In perceiving this aspect of language, with the sense of speech sounds, we are concerned with feeling rather than thought, and indeed we can enjoy the speech sounds of languages of which we don't understand a word. Into the speech sounds there also flow the individual's own intonation and feelings, which 'move' us in various ways. With the help of our sense of speech sounds, we dance a little inwardly with the words we hear, using a meta-morphosed sense of movement turned away from our own movements to apprehend the movement, as also the colour, mood and 'emotion', in the speech of another.

It is important to realise that the sense of speech sounds is not particularly concerned with the conceptual meaning these sounds may bear (except in so far as some words bear something of their meanings within the sounds themselves – 'thus', 'snake', 'rush', 'sting' etc.). To discern the thoughts borne by the words we need the sense of thought. How can we try to understand this sense as a kind of turning inside out of the sense of life? The latter is concerned with perception of the harmony or disharmony of our organic processes. These processes are essentially organised rhythms. With our sense of life we perceive how the stream of rhythmic time-processes is well-organised or ill-organised.

The physical medium by which thoughts are borne to us is also a pattern of organised movement. This may be the pattern or organisation – the *sequence* of movement – in a stream of speech sounds. Or it may be the sequence of gesture-movements made by a skilled mime (who may be able to convey remarkably complex thoughts in this way. Here, again, it is important to recognise that the *sense* of thought does not give us the thought *content*, but only the physical vehicle, the stream of organised living movement in speech or gesture, into which a content can flow. We ourselves search inwardly for the content – for the concepts which belong to the perceived speech sounds and organised pattern of speech flow. (This distinction applies to all the senses; they give us percepts which are themselves without 'meaning' until we find the corresponding concepts.)

Thus we may begin to understand the sense of thought as a perception of the 'life form' of the thoughts themselves which someone is trying to convey to us, apprehended by a sense of life turned outward from immersion in the organised flow of our bodily life processes, in order to apprehend the 'thought life' of another.

Finally, and perhaps most difficult of all, is the search for a clear awareness of the sense of the 'I' of another person. When we use the word 'tact' we indicate that in the meeting of two people there is a kind of delicate, non-physical touching. But it is not easy to become more aware of what the perception actually is. It can be helpful to recollect, soon afterwards, a first meeting with someone. There will be memories of what was said, of a physical appearance, emotional reactions, etc. But if all these are put aside, and one asks what is left, there may remain an impression which is best described as a kind of 'force-form', as though one had 'touched', very dimly, the essential *will* of the person one has met.

It is particularly with these three senses that the problems of truth and illusion become most acute (the more so because their very existence is not generally recognised). They already arise clearly with sight and hearing: we never normally say 'I could not believe my balance'; but we often say that we could not believe our eyes or ears.

Much more serious, though, is the 'alienation' which leads to doubt and distrust in every human encounter. Many people will remember vividly sudden moments of such doubt, probably in their ninth year, when children begin for the first time to feel separate, alone and perhaps surrounded by strangers. Such moments pass, but often return strongly with adolescence. The healthy side of this is an acute sense for the integrity or otherwise of those around, and a sharp nose for what is 'phoney' (except that it is not the nose, but the senses of 'I', thought and word which are particularly involved). But if this awakening to separateness becomes extreme, it may bring cynicism, chronic distrust and an inability as an adult to 'make contact' with other human beings – a contact which depends on a proper functioning of the senses of word, thought and 'I'.

It is probable that some elements of indulgence or illusion can touch every one of the twelve senses. Nevertheless, it seems clear that the problematic aspect of the senses which most concerned the East – attachment and entanglement in 'self' and in earthly existence – arises mainly in connection with the six bodily or 'self-centred' senses. In the West, we have gained great confidence in the science of bodies, in grasping mass, motion, position, etc., with mathematical certainty. It is a certainty born out of the establishment of an inner security in our own bodies, in early childhood, as we learn to stand, walk and manipulate the objects around us. (Certain lines of research in child development are beginning to reveal what Steiner pointed to over fifty years ago, namely that the apparently abstract mathematical thinking of later life is deeply at work, although unconsciously, in small children learning to know the world of bodies.) At the same time, we are deeply uncertain about any realities outside our capacity to touch, weigh, measure and manipulate – so much so, that they may be banished to an inaccessible realm of 'things in themselves' (as with Kant, or in the case of spiritual realities to a realm accessible only to faith.

The division in the sphere of the twelve senses is reflected in the split between 'science and religion', and the emergence of a kind of empirical and manipulative knowledge working with 'laws of nature', but empty of *moral* laws.

It is therefore not surprising that it is the West, particularly, which has produced a body-centred, consumer society, plundering the earth to assuage disordered appetites, while at the same time experiencing an increasing emptiness of moral life and human relationships, and a deep uncertainty about the meaning of existence.

I mentioned earlier the need for a 'therapy' of the senses. I believe that we can begin to see our way if we take a new look at the whole sphere of the senses, not dualistically, but as a threefold structure. Rudolf Steiner often classified the twelve senses in this way also, speaking of four 'will' senses (touch, life, movement, balance), four 'feeling' senses (smell, taste, sight, warmth), and four 'spiritual' senses (hearing, word, thought, 'I').

In Steiner's recommendations for three main phases of education – nursery, lower school and upper school – we can glimpse a remarkable kind of nurture of the twelve senses. He wanted the nursery and kindergarten to be full of practical activities – baking, cleaning, washing up, making things out of simple materials – but activities filled with reverence and care for the substances and things of the surroundings. Here the qualities of the substances, materials and furniture matter greatly – perhaps more than at any other time.

Small children, Steiner sometimes said, are completely united with the whole sphere of their sense-perceptions, which is less differentiated than in adults. Because of this they are deeply imitative – everything in the surroundings makes a deep inner impression. Small children have no possibility of 'alienating' themselves from their surroundings (except in tragic disorders of autism and the like). Thus they 'imitate' the very qualities of the things around them, so it is crucial that these should be 'honest'. An object which is a kind of a lie – which is in any way fake, or made of materials estranged from nature – brings a kind of immorality to the child through his senses. The traditions and instincts of true *craftmanship* are needed above all in the creation of the environment to nourish the senses of young children. The children, Steiner once said, should be able to experience at this time 'the world is *good*'. This is the source for true security and inner certainty in the world in later life, and for the birth of the real creative moral being of the individual working in the will.

In the lower school, from six to fourteen, a great demand is made on the class teacher. He or she must strive to be above all an *artist*. For the emotional life of children is awakened in a new way, with a sense for drama, the battle of good and evil, beauty and ugliness. Here all the arts are needed, and here, too, lie the strongest and most comprehensive possibilities for a nourishment and therapy of all twelve senses. The plastic arts – sculpture, modelling, woodwork, etc. – engage particularly the will senses, but relate these activities also to the life of feeling. The arts involving music and language (including drama and poetry) engage particularly the spiritual senses of hearing, word, thought and 'I' but again embracing them into the sphere of feeling. Quite centrally stands painting, the art which lives with colour, but into which play subtly our senses of taste, smell and warmth.

It is at this time, above all, when a kind of bridge can be created, so that the child learns to breathe freely between himself and the surrounding world. And it is in the arts that the most crucial therapy for the enlivening and healing of the senses lies. In the middle school, Steiner said, the child must experience 'the world is *beautiful*'.

In the upper school, the pupils are faced with a new kind of challenge. They meet teachers in a new way, as 'knowers', as 'scientists' in the true sense, specialists in different fields of knowledge. The task here is to open the world to the pupils as it lives in the experience and enthusiasm of adults. In adolescence, a more detached perception begins; the spheres of sense perception and inner life begin to be more distinguished, and among other things pupils begin to take a more objective look at their teachers and parents, and to realise that they are by no means perfect. But adolescents are always searching for true perceptions mediated by the spiritual senses of word, thought and 'I', for the truth in the human beings around them.

The confusion of untruthful images and violent or chaotic music with which our culture assaults adolescents at this time is a direct attack on the senses, but particularly on the spiritual senses which are most crucial for building a true understanding between man and man. Here again, we must seek for therapies in all the arts, but perhaps particularly in drama, poetry and song.

A deeper understanding of the senses will also open the way to new science, in which the senses can be trusted because they are known in their different functions and qualities. In the upper school, adolescents will be greatly helped by teachers who can show them a path of devoted and exact observation of natural phenomena. In this connection, Steiner pointed often to the path taken by Goethe, which enabled him to discover the 'Ur-plant', the archetypal plant present formatively in the plants around him – an Idea perceived in reality. This is the path for the healing and overcoming of alienation. In the upper school, Steiner said, the pupils should come to experience 'the word is *true*'.

I began this essay by exploring the role of the senses in waking up, a birth out of the womb of sleep into the light of day. Growing up entails a related birth and awakening, for which home and school provide a womb. If human beings are to awaken to themselves in the world, they need the freedom of a healthy sphere of twelve senses. To help this is one of the central tasks of the education initiated by Rudolf Steiner. But it is a task which needs to continue throughout adult life. In practical terms, it means working for an environment in which the 'goodness' of the crafts, the beauty of the arts, and the truth of the sciences interweave.

The birth of our true humanity thus depends on the right nourishment through the 'well-springs' of our senses as essentially as on the air we breathe and the food we eat. But we need also to become aware of the 'monsters' which lurk in these well-springs. I have already mentioned the kind that would enslave us in greed and addiction, and fetter us permanently to the world of bodies. But there are also the monsters that would alienate us, abstract us from reality and take us wandering in worlds of private inner fantasy because we can find no secure relation to the surrounding world and other people, or do not wish to come down to earth.

In the whole spectrum of the arts, which (as we have seen) can weave through all our senses, we can begin to bring the different spheres of perception into a more living and weaving relationship, as the rainbow makes a bridge between heaven and earth. We need to bring something of the realism and certainty which is given naturally through the body-senses into the world of our spiritual senses, while these need to lend some of their essential 'selflessness' to the will-senses.

Through our four feeling-senses we are linked quite particularly with the world of nature: with colour, the warmth of the sun, the tastes and smells of the plants and animals which feed us. We have developed a civilisation which in its knowing is estranged from nature, and in its doing is destroying nature. The therapy must begin with a sense of gratitude and wonder to the nourishment that is given by nature, through our twelve senses, so that we may awaken to ourselves, and to our responsibilities on earth.

1975

From *Hope, Evolution and Change*
John Davy, Hawthorn Press, 1983

[1] In *Anthroposophie: ein Fragment* (Rudolf Steiner Nachlassverwaltung, 1970). Not yet translated.
[2] We may object that we hear birdsong 'coming from a bird'. But that is an interpretation, added by thinking, to the sensation itself. The actual percept is simply 'given', as are all sense-perceptions, simply by waking up and becoming open to sense-experience. For a fuller discussion of this crucial point, see Rudolf Steiner's *Philosophy of Freedom*. (Rudolf Steiner Press, 1964).
[3] It is extremely difficult, and a subject of much current scientific debate, to disentangle the physiological and the psychological components of pain experience.
[4] *Man as a Being of Sense and Perception*, three lectures, Dornach, July, 1921. (Rudolf Steiner Press; out of print).

Appendix II

The School of Spiritual Psychology

The School of Spiritual Psychology seeks to assist individuals in the development of conscious soul capacities and receptivity to the reality of the spiritual worlds. Such development serves as a force of positive change in the world, oriented toward forming a spiritual culture.

Spiritual Psychology unites the highest (spirit) with the deepest (soul) and views the individual as the chalice of this union. This endeavor might aptly be called a GRAIL PSYCHOLOGY. It coordinates the inner life with soul and spirit qualities of the outer world and recognises that individual development is not for one's sake alone, but for the Earth, the World, and the Community.

The particular approach to questions of soul, spirit, and world taken by the School of Spiritual Psychology derives from a creative synthesis of phenomenological psychology, the Depth Psychology of C. G. Jung and its extension into Archetypal Psychology, and the Spiritual Science of Rudolf Steiner.

The School of Spiritual Psychology holds the view that psychology is not the exclusive province of the professional, and that an education into soul and spirit is a necessity in order to be a full human being. To this end, a variety of ways to enter into taking responsibility for one's inner life are offered by the School.

The School of Spiritual Psychology provides the following services:

Ongoing Courses and Seminars in various parts of the country, initiated by individuals wishing to bring this work to their communities. Plans are underway to begin a residential program.

Correspondence Courses and a program of studies leading to the Master's and Ph.D in spiritual psychology through Greenwich University.

A yearly International Sophia Conference, offered each summer.

Individual lectures bring the work of the School to bear on the renewal of various professions such as education, medicine, psychotherapy, and business.

Consulting with individuals, organizations, and institutions wishing to bring practical spiritual change to their endeavors.

The Center for Sacred Service of the School of Spiritual Psychology provides seminars concerning keeping soul and spirit central in efforts to be of help to others in their activity; development of contemplation as the threshold between soul and spirit experiences; an orientation toward meditation; exercises for observing the world; the method of phenomenological description; working with dreams in a non-interpretive manner; conversations on healthy inner development.

Readings include:
Dennis Kolcek, *Seeking Spirit Vision;*
Rudolf Steiner, *How to Know Higher Worlds;*
and selections from the writings of C. G. Jung on Alchemical imagination and active imagination

Advanced Seminars
The Advanced Seminars of the School of Spiritual Psychology are offered in two formats; they can he presented in a form that does not require the Foundation Series and stand independently as topics of concern for individuals interested in the unique perspective of Spiritual Psychology; they are also presented in a format for those individuals who have participated in the Foundation Series and wish to continue to deepen their study, research, and inner development. In the latter case, more depth of presentation is provided along with further and more extended exercises.

Care of the Senses: The Art of Soulful Living
One of the most important contributions made by Rudolf Steiner
was his description of the existence of twelve senses. This seminar
explores how to attend to each of these sensory capacities in
healthy ways. How we are in danger of losing the soul dimension
of sensing is presented, and the gifts of each of the senses
described. How imbalances in sensing relate to disorders such as
dyslexia, hyperactivity, anxiety, depression is explored. The relation
between sensory numbness to the development of addictions is
presented. Practical suggestions and exercises for soulfully culti-
vating a re-enchantment of the sensory worlds and care of the
senses in daily living form a central aspect of the seminar.

Spiritual Psychology and the Soul of Sensing
The human senses form the exquisite tapestry of the body, weaving the wonders of the world into the folds of inner life. There is
no way to live soulfully in the world without first being deliciously
immersed in it. The modern world is in danger of forgetting the
beauty of the world – the world of natural color, sound, rhythm,
taste, touch. The neglect of the senses, their lack of healthy cultiva-
tion, results in a society hungry for sense experience, but without
the means of discriminating between healthy and harmful sensory
experiences. This course seeks to develop the capacities to be awake
and aware in sensing.

Lesson 1
An introduction to the nature of the twelve senses. These senses,
working in a particular kind of harmony, are distinguished and
grouped, and the nature of the grouping discussed. Relations to
other forms that occur in 'twelves' are discussed, particularly the
Zodiac. In addition, we look at the 12 senses in relation to the 7
life processes.

Lesson 2
A consideration of the four senses related to body awareness.
These senses – touch, the life sense. movement, and balance, are
the most primary senses, through which we establish the experience

of our body. A phenomenological description of each of these senses and their importance is given and exercises for helping to discern the particular soul qualities invoked with each are suggested.

Lesson 3
A consideration of the four middle, or alchemical senses – warmth, smell, taste, and vision. These are the senses through which we come to know the world around us in all its wonder and diversity. These senses are also the ones in which a creative exchange goes on between our body and the surrounding world. Exercises are given to develop the soul qualities of these senses. Descriptions of the cultural evolution of these senses is given.

Lesson 4
The spiritual senses – hearing, the speech sense, the thought sense, and the 'I' sense. Except for hearing, this group of senses is relatively unknown in our time, but they will prove increasingly crucial as a path to the healing of the senses concerned with body awareness. Descriptions of each of these senses is given, along with exercises to develop these sense capacities.

Lesson 5
An exploration of the disruptions of the four bodily senses and the individual, social, and cultural ramifications of these disruptions. Some of the areas in which these disruptions have dire effects, including education, religion, politics, economics, and medicine, are explored. The relation of disruptions of these senses to fear, anxiety, depression, attention deficit disorder, dyslexia and other psychological difficulties are presented.

Lesson 6
Descriptions of disruption in the middle realm of sensing, the alchemical senses. How disruptions in these realms disturbs the development of relationships with others and with the world is described. A reflection on the importance of becoming conscious in these senses and some methods for developing this capacity; the significance of disturbances in these senses as affecting artistic ability.

Lesson 7
How disruptions in the development of these senses affect the development of the capacities to communicate, relate to others selflessly, and to create are considered. The origins of destructive behavior as originating in disturbances in the development of these senses.

Lesson 8
Healing the disruptions of the senses. This lesson focuses on the relation of the spiritual senses to the body senses and how proper development of the spiritual senses can bring about healing of imbalances in the body senses. A consideration of the importance of these relationships in the education of children.

Lesson 9
Healing the disruptions of the alchemical senses; the creativity of these senses; the arts as a necessity rather than a luxury; the particular art forms that bring healing to each of these senses; meditations and exercises for these senses.

Lesson 10
How we are held captive in our culture by forces that prevail against 'coming to our senses'; breaking free of our own traps of thinking and value structures that bind the senses: The cultural forms that hinder and those that enhance healthy sensing.

Lesson 11
Sensing and beauty; the beauty of the natural world; the uplifting of the senses through the arts: the 12 senses and 12 art forms; the necessity of beauty for health; the healing power of beauty.

Lesson 12
Prayers to the senses. From a sense of freedom to a sense of destiny, to the capacity to trust, love, give, and even be present to our own conscience, the senses form the foundation of the most deeply human qualities of our being; this lesson develops prayers for the development of the gifts of the senses, ways of speaking to and listening to the wisdom of the senses.

THE SCHOOL OF SPIRITUAL PSYCHOLOGY
is co-directed by:

Robert Sardello, Ph.D
Faculty member of the Dallas Institute of Humanities and Culture, Texas, and the Chalice of Repose Project, Missoula, Montana. Former chairman of the Department of Psychology, University of Dallas. A practicing psychotherapist for over twenty years, working in Jungian and Archetypal Psychology. Developed a Spiritual Psychology based in the Spiritual Science of Rudolf Steiner. Has taught courses at Emerson College, Schumaker College, The Goethean Studies program of Rudolf Steiner College, the Rudolf Steiner Institute. Author of *Facing the World with Soul, Love and the Soul, Freeing the Soul From Fear.*

Cheryl L. Sanders, MS
Worked as an addiction counselor, teacher, working in public agencies and private practice for 28 years. Co-founded programs in Perinatal Intervention in Dallas, Texas and conducts workshops on forming community coalitions for women and minority groups for health and human services. Published children's stories as guided for teaching about AIDS and substance abuse. Conducts workshops for faculties and parents dealing with teaching about abuse, violence, AIDS, and addictive behavior. Published in the area of sensory awareness for children and for adults. Completing doctoral dissertation on the Spiritual Psychology of Sensing.

Ordering books

If you have difficulties ordering Hawthorn Press books from a bookshop, you can order online at **www.hawthornpress.com** or you can order direct from:

United Kingdom

Booksource 32 Finlas Street, Glasgow, G22 5DU
Tel: (08702) 402182 Fax: (0141) 557 0189
Email: orders@booksource.net

USA/North America

SteinerBooks PO Box 960, Herndon, VA 20172-0960
Tel: (800) 856 8664 Fax: (703) 661 1501
Email: service@steinerbooks.org